Your Story

Get Unstuck, Reach Your Goals, &
Become the Empowered Author of Your Life

DAN TECK

DandiLove Unlimited

Printed in the United States of America
ISBN-13: 978-0-9981251-3-8

To Jodi,
with my infinite love and gratitude for sharing this journey
and co-authoring our never-ending love story.

Also, heartfelt thanks to everyone who has inspired me—on the page and
beyond—including my wise and wonderful teachers, fellow writers in the
Your Soulful Book community, everyone who shared their stories for this
book, and the too-many-to-name authors whose words have informed my
own, touched my heart, and changed my life.

CONTENTS

Rewriting Your Life

We only have one life, but we can choose
what kind of story it's going to be.
— Rick Riordan

M Y FRIEND TONY AND I have been having the same conversation for the last ten years. We only talk every few months, but it always feels like just a few minutes have gone by because he keeps repeating the same old story: "I'm tired of my job. My boss is driving me crazy. I want to quit and start my own business. And write a book. And get in shape. And move out west. But I'm not in a position financially to give up my salary, plus my wife would throw a fit. Besides, there's no time for any of this—between work and the kids and family obligations on the weekends…and then it all starts again Monday morning. Plus, I can't seem to kick this cold."

I love Tony, but I'm sick of his story. And I know *he* is too—because he tells me so…every single time we talk!

Do you know anyone like Tony—someone who sounds like a broken record? Every time you talk to them, they say the same old thing over and over. Sure, some of the details change, but the underlying story is the same. Maybe their story is that they're too busy. Or they're having health problems. Or they're fed up with their job or their spouse or their family. Maybe they have a big dream they never realize, or they just feel a vague sense of dissatisfaction with their life in general. And the most frustrating part is that they never seem to do anything about it; they just keep on telling and living that same old tired story…over and over and over—day after day, month after month, year after year.

Do you ever feel this way in your own life? Do you ever find yourself repeating the same old patterns in your relationships, career, family, or other areas of life? Do you find yourself having the same arguments, facing the same frustrations, feeling the same emotions, and ending up in the same situations…again and again and again? Do you wish you could stop your unhealthy habits, break out of your ruts, and live the life you want instead of the life you've got?

If so, don't worry—it's not just you and Tony who feel this way. Lots of us have been there—including me. I've felt the frustration of being miles away from the life I wanted. I've spent years spinning my wheels in a self-created rut. I've repeated the same bad habits, told the same disempowering stories, and gotten the same results (or non-results) so many times that I sometimes felt like I was stuck in the movie *Groundhog Day*, living the same day over and over. Sure, the details changed, but the underlying story was the same: *Not enough time. Not enough money. Too busy. Too tired. Running myself ragged, struggling just to get by, and putting my dreams on hold…indefinitely.*

One painful story I told myself (year after year after year) was that I didn't have time to realize my #1 dream: to finish and publish my book. This failure was made even more painful (and embarrassing) by the fact that I was coaching others to write, finish, and publish *their* books while my own seemingly never-ending work in progress languished in a purgatory of unrealized dreams. I felt like a hypocrite and a fraud.

The worst part of all was that I told (and lived) this story for so long that I started to feel like I was stuck in it forever, like things would never change—like I would die with my music (and my books) still inside me.

Eventually, though, I realized that not only could I change my story, but I already had the tools to do so—the same ones I'd been using for decades as a writer and editor: identifying less-than-ideal aspects of characters and situations, deleting the parts that didn't work, building on the good stuff, and rewriting the story the way I wanted it to be. I'd already used this process to change dozens of fictional stories; why not use it to change the story of my real life? It was certainly worth a shot.

So, did it work? Did these tools help me escape the ruts I'd been in, enjoy my life, feel better about myself, and reach my "happy ending"? The fact that you're reading this published book is Exhibit A (or "Exhibit B" for *book*) that yes, these tools do work. And they're not just helpful with writing. In the six years since I began to consciously apply the "RYS" (Rewrite Your Story) method, almost every part of my life has improved: I've gone from struggling just to get by to living in abundance. I moved from a house right next to a construction site (in a town I felt no connection with) to a beautiful home three minutes from the beach. I do more of what I love, spend more time in nature, more time with my furry friends, and more time with my wife. And, beyond external goals, I feel more like myself—living my true life—than ever before.

After finding success with these tools in my own life, I also began using them with life-coaching clients, authors, and others, helping them reach their own dreams—even when they had nothing to do with books or writing. And I know that the writer's toolbox can work magic in your life as well, regardless of what your aspirations may be.

Using fiction-writing techniques to improve your real life may seem odd at first, but it actually works—and it makes a lot of sense. After all, our goals aren't that different from those of the great heroes in books and stories through the centuries: ultimately, we all want to satisfy our desires, live our calling, transform our lives, feel better about ourselves (and in general), touch the people we love in meaningful ways, and know that our lives matter.

But unlike all those fictional heroes, we're not stuck in someone else's book, left to the mercy of an external author. We are the authors of our own stories! We simply need to claim our power, pick up the pen, and write the happy ending (and middle, and right-now) we so richly deserve and desire.

So, are you ready to turn your life into a masterpiece? If so, read on and get ready to dive into the RYS method, step into your power, and change your story…and your life. I can't wait to see the amazing story you'll create.

Happy writing, rewriting, and living!

– Dan

The Story of Your Story

We often live out the stories we've been told, sometimes without questioning the truthfulness of them. [However,] at any point in your story, you are free to reimagine the narrative you are living.
— Jeff Goins

ONCE UPON A TIME, someone told you a flawed story that took root inside you and determined the course of your life.

You first heard this story when you were very young—maybe about seven years old (or three, thirteen, nineteen, or any other impressionable age). The story might have come from parents, siblings, friends, peers, society, the media, a casual acquaintance, or someone you didn't even know. It might have even come from your younger self's interpretation of childhood experiences. The storytelling may have been direct (through someone's words) or indirect (through their actions—or their *reactions* to you as they reinforced or discouraged certain words and behaviors). It might have been as overt as a lengthy lecture or as subtle as a raised eyebrow; but one way or another, the message got across. The seed was planted, and the story took root.

And although it was a deeply flawed story told from a very limited perspective, you were so young that you accepted this story as absolute truth. And you repeated it. You told it to yourself. You told it to others. And you acted it out (adapting the story into the movie of your life, so to speak). And the more you told it and acted it out, the more you reinforced it—and the more it came true.

That story—initially told to and then told *by* a child—began to steer your thoughts and actions in a less-than-ideal direction, as if a seven-year-old were driving the car of your life. And, as you'd expect from a seven-year-old driving a car, the story wreaked havoc on your life. But by then you were so accustomed to it that you hardly noticed. The story even provided an odd sense of comfort and familiarity. No, it didn't serve your highest self or lead to your best potential life, but there was nothing that could be done. That's just the way it was. This story was your truth, your reality, your life.

What's the Story?

So, what is the story you heard at that impressionable age—the one that has stuck with you all these years and caused so many problems?

It might be something someone told you about yourself: Maybe they said you weren't that smart or that pretty, or that you weren't good with numbers or with art, or that you were clumsy and accident prone, or that you were selfish, or that you'd never amount to much.

Or maybe someone told you an "if-then" story: If you want to be successful, then you have to work very hard and sacrifice a lot. If you don't have kids, you're being selfish. If a woman wants to find a good husband, she has to be beautiful. If a man wants to find a good wife, he has to be rich. If you get too successful ("too big for your britches"), you'll become an elitist snob. If you pursue your passion, you'll never make much money.

Maybe a parent or another relative told you a story about your family: We're honest people who work with our hands. We never have much money, but we make enough to get by. The women in this family are prone to illness. The men in this family are all scoundrels. We don't air our dirty laundry—what happens in this house stays in this house.

Maybe you heard a story about a certain area of life, such as love, politics, education, money, or spirituality: Relationships are hard. Republicans are heartless and greedy. Democrats are lazy freeloaders. If you want to be successful, you have to go to a private college. If you go to a private college, you'll be cloistered in an ivory tower and lose touch with the real world. Rich people aren't spiritual, and spiritual people aren't rich.

Or maybe you heard a story about all people or the world in general: It's a dog-eat-dog world. Nice guys finish last. You can't teach an old dog new tricks. No pain, no gain. There's always a catch. Life's a bitch and then you die.

What's *Your* Story?

Have you heard any of these stories? Are you *living* any of them? Or do you have a completely different but equally powerful story? Or maybe you're not sure what your story is…or if you even have one.

I don't know what your story is, but I can guarantee that you have one! There's no shame in that—*everyone* has a story. You might just not notice yours because you've been telling it and living with it for so long that it's become invisible to you. You may be too close to see it at all (even if it's clear to others—like spinach in your teeth). Or maybe you've so fully accepted it as universal truth that you don't even think of it as a story—much less *your* story. But it's still part of your life. More than that: it's *controlling* your life, for better or worse (probably for worse).

No matter what your story is, this book will help you discover it and do something about it! It will help you reclaim the steering wheel of your life and start heading in the direction you actually want to go. It will help you write the story you want to live…and turn your life into the masterpiece you deserve.

What's the Big Deal?

Why is it so important to figure out your story, and why do you need to do anything about it? What's the big deal? After all, it's just a story—and maybe even a *good* story, right?

Yes! Some stories are very good—meaning that they support your highest self in living your best, happiest, most fulfilled life—stories such as: "I'm a highly capable, intelligent person who has the power to create the life of my dreams" or "The universe conspires to support me." If you have a story like this, by all means, hold on to it! But those are not the kind of stories we're focusing on in this book (at least not at first). Those are not the ones we want to rewrite. Those are the stories we want to embrace, celebrate, and live to the fullest!

And yes, all stories—even those that aren't 100% positive (meaning that they have elements that block your potential)—have some benefits: They offer you a sense of belonging (connecting you with others who are living the same story) or individuation (distinguishing you from those who are living a different story). Also, the more you live a story, the more your experiences reinforce it and "make you right" (through the nearly universal phenomenon of *confirmation bias*), which can feel pretty good! And the longer your story sticks around, the more familiar it becomes and the more it provides a sense of security, identity, continuity, and comfort ("that stealthy thing that enters the house a guest, and then becomes a host, and then a master," as Kahlil Gibran wrote).

Over time, though, a disempowering story's apparent benefits are the very things that trap you in a life that doesn't serve your best interests or help you reach your potential. Eventually, you no longer live in the world; you live in your story. And you no longer experience your life; you experience your story. It surrounds you. It controls you. It imprisons you.

This is the kind of story we're focusing on in this book—the kind we want to rewrite in order to free ourselves from its snares and transform our lives.

For instance, let's say you've bought into the story that the world is a scary place and people can't be trusted (perhaps stemming from a well-meaning parent who warned you about strangers). If you never rewrite this story, you could very well go through every day of your life feeling scared—always looking over your shoulder, half expecting someone to stab you in the back (figuratively or literally)—and end up loveless, alone, and plagued by stress-related health issues.

Or let's say you've bought into a negative story about yourself, such as "I'm a starter but not a finisher." This simple statement could lead to decades of chronic frustration and dissatisfaction as you fail to reach one goal after another until the end of your life, when you look back and realize that you never accomplished what was most important to you.

As you read the first part of this book (in which you'll discover and/or clarify your story), you'll see just how much your story affects your life. But even if you're not yet sure what your story is, you can try this thought experiment with any recurring thought, action, belief, or statement that *might* be part of your story. Consider its impact on your present life, then take it a step further: extrapolate until the end of your life (as the Ghost of Christmas Future did with Scrooge) and ask yourself:

- Does the path of this story lead to a place I actually want to go, or does it lead to a dead end (or to a circular rut that just goes around and around and around the same unappealing track)?
- What ruts might I get (and *stay*) stuck in if I continue to let this story determine my life path?
- What opportunities will I miss if I don't follow another story-path?
- What potential will never be realized?
- What "music" (passion, project, talent, or dream) will die inside me?
- What joy, satisfaction, and love might I miss out on because of this story?

I realize that answering these questions may very well lead to some pretty bleak visions. And while I hate to be a downer, I have to be honest and tell you that these bleak visions will become your reality…unless you rewrite your story!

But you can't rewrite your story until you expose the lie at the heart of the story…and embrace the antidote to that lie.

The Lie at the Heart of the Story

Your story might be completely false—based on a mistake, a misunderstanding, or a mean-spirited lie. Most likely, however, there is an element of truth to it (albeit not the *whole* truth). But no matter how true parts of your story may be, at its heart is a pernicious lie:

You have no choice in the matter—that's just the way it is.

It's almost as if someone told you that you're just a character stuck in someone else's story rather than the author of your own story. But nothing could be further from the truth! Because, no matter how deeply enmeshed you are in your story, you always have one essential thing that sets you apart from a character (which is also the key to freedom and the antidote to the lie at the heart of the story):

Choice

No matter what type of book a character is in—be it literary fiction, romance, mystery/thriller, or sci-fi/adventure—every character has one thing in common: they're at the mercy of their author. They lack free will.

You, on the other hand, always have a choice in your life. You get to create your own character. You have autonomy, freedom, and the power of self-determination. You get to write the scenes you live. And if you don't like something about your story, you get to change it…and write the happy ending (and middle and present) you've always dreamed of!

Once you claim this "author-ity" over your own life, you no longer have to live an outdated story written by your younger self. You can live a new, healthier story written by your empowered higher self who knows that you can be the hero of your own story—you just have to use your power, pick up the pen, and write the story the way you want it to be…as opposed to the way it's always been written.

What Do I Mean by "Rewrite Your Story"?

First of all, by "your story," I don't mean every last detail of your life. (This is not a creative-writing primer or a book about how to write your memoir.) When I refer to "your story" here, I'm not just talking about externals: where you grew up, how many siblings you have, or where you work (although these may be elements of your story). I'm talking about the experiences, relationships, dynamics, characteristics, and core beliefs that define you:

- The story you tell over and over again (to others or even just to yourself—within your own mind)
- The story you *live* over and over again
- The story that has a thousand variations that all share the same underlying premise, dynamics, and structure
- The story that's so close to you that you may not even realize it's a story

- The story that's so integrally wrapped up in your life that it feels like you're stuck in it
- The story that feels like it's your life
- The story that feels like you

When I talk about rewriting this story, I don't mean denying or lying about your past. In this book, "rewriting" means framing your past in the most empowering way, gaining awareness about your present (especially the choices available to you), and exercising your creative right to design your future the way you want to—remembering that your future does not have to look like your past.

If you're tired of your old story (either the whole thing or any part of it), know that you don't have to stay stuck in it. The time has come to write a new chapter—or a whole new story—for your life.

Better Story, Better Life

If you're open to this process and you honestly engage with the exercises on the pages to come, by the time you finish this book, you will have changed an old negative story that doesn't serve you into one that reflects your highest self. For instance:

- "I'll never amount to anything" might be rewritten as "Because I get to write my own story and create my own life experience, I can achieve my goals and live my dreams."
- "If I pursue my passion, I'll never make much money" might be rewritten as "By doing what I love, I open the door to unlimited abundance—emotionally and financially."
- "You can't teach an old dog new tricks" might be rewritten as "As long as I'm alive, I can keep learning, growing, and expanding my horizons."

In fact, this last rewritten story is a good place to start since it's a prerequisite for this entire process—there's not much point embarking on this journey unless you believe that you can and will learn, grow, and change! This really is the premise of the whole book: you're not stuck. You can and will rewrite your story and change your life.

How It Works

So, how do you write a new story for your life? By using the same steps that novelists, short-story authors, and screenwriters go through when they write a story: brainstorming, freewriting, drafting, editing, and publishing. The only difference between you and a fiction writer is that instead of dealing with made-up characters and situations, you'll go through this process with the story of your actual life, and then you'll take your new story beyond the page and actually *live* it! Also, unlike published books (which generally remain the same—word for word—after they're published), your story is a living, breathing thing that you get to edit, adapt, or rewrite any time you want for as long as you live.

To make this process fun and manageable, I've divided it into four parts:

1. *Identify Your Story* – Recognize which stories you keep retelling and reliving, identify the "master story" at the root of these smaller stories, and see how it's controlling you and how you can break free from it.
2. *Release Your Story* – Let go of old stories, labels, worldviews, and patterns that aren't serving you, while keeping the ones that do serve you and making room for new ones that help you live your best life.
3. *Rewrite Your Story* – Create a story that empowers you and reflects your highest self.
4. *Live Your Story* – Reinforce the new story and make it a living, breathing part of your everyday life.

Throughout the book, I'll share the creative-writing tools and techniques I've learned as a writer, combined with life-changing personal-growth exercises and perspectives that have helped me, my life-coaching clients, and many others in all areas of life. I'll also share real-life examples of people who rewrote their stories (and some who didn't) and how it changed their lives (or didn't).

Unlike most books or movies that are designed to be passively read or watched, this book is an interactive, hands-on, full-participation experience—full of thought-provoking, soul-searching, and (hopefully) enjoyable exercises that focus on practical application. The goal here isn't to learn a bunch of abstract theories—it's to actually write and *live* a new story.

This is why I really, *really, REALLY* encourage you to do the exercises (set apart in gray boxes)—to write down your responses to the questions and literally write and rewrite your story. You may find it easiest to use a separate notebook, but please feel free to write directly in this book. However, I realize that not everyone is going to take the time to do this. (I admit that I've frequently read self-help books without writing down the exercise responses. Hey, we've all done it—there's no shame in it!) But even if you don't write your responses, I encourage you to at least read the questions and answer them in your own mind. This way, you'll still be engaging with this material, internalizing it, and making the process your own.

Your Move

So now it's up to you to decide: Will you keep on spinning your wheels, living your same old story, getting the same old results (or *lack* of results)? Or will you claim your power to create a better story and a better life? If an old friend calls you a month from now, a year from now, or a decade from now, will they think what I do every time I talk to Tony: "You're still in exactly the same place as you were a year ago—different details, same old story"? Or will they think, "Wow! You're really soaring"?

The choice is yours. Will you put off changing your story until tomorrow (or a distant "someday" that never seems to arrive), or will you start creating the future you want *right now*? I hope you'll choose to soar—to change, grow, claim your power, embrace your freedom, and take the first step toward the life you desire and deserve. If your heart is urging you to take this step, then turn the page, pull out a pen, and get ready to write (and learn and grow and have fun) and rewrite your story!

PART I

Identify Your Story

Almost all of us have a story about why we don't access our genius. When we are within that story, it is very difficult to know that it's just a story.
– Gay Hendricks

CHAPTER ONE

Stories with Consequences

*It is almost impossible to make decisions that don't reinforce
the story about who you believe yourself to be.*
— Bernadette Jiwa

I RECENTLY GOT AN EMAIL from a woman who told me a powerful story: she said she's unlovable because she's flawed. This might not seem like much of a story, but it's actually two stories in one:

1. No one can love me.
2. In order for someone to be lovable, they have to be flawless.

She had watched an interview of me discussing relationships and wanted my advice for finding a romantic partner. I offered her about half a dozen suggestions I thought might be helpful, but if I'd had to limit myself to just three words, they would have been this book's title: *Rewrite Your Story*. Until she does this, it's hard to imagine anyone getting past the impenetrable barrier to love she's built around herself.

And it's not just her romantic life that's affected by this story. It closes the door to love of *all* kinds. It also wreaks havoc on her self-esteem, which hurts her work, her social interactions, her creative endeavors, and just about anything else she might do…or *not* do because she lacks the confidence to try it. And it robs her of would-be satisfaction in all areas of life because her self-imposed requirement of flawlessness sets her up for chronic disappointment rather than allowing her to enjoy the beauty of "good enough" or "perfectly imperfect."

It pains me to contemplate how much she's suffered just because of this one-line story. And it pains me even more to think about the suffering she might experience throughout the rest of her life if she doesn't change this story. I can imagine her near the end of her life, looking back at so many wasted years, filled with regret over the connections she never made, the opportunities she never took advantage of, and the love she never experienced. I can imagine the remorse she'd feel about wasting so much time on self-criticism that caused her so much unnecessary stress and robbed her of so much potential joy. I can feel her big-picture disappointment and the moment-by-moment sadness of going through life with such low self-esteem—feeling unloved and unlovable.

I know that this woman isn't the only one having this type of experience. We all have stories of one kind or another—stories that affect us on a daily basis and determine the course of our lives. And while some of them are positive and life affirming, many of them cause us needless suffering. Some stories are clearly a big deal (such as "I'm unlovable"), but others might seem small and innocuous, such as one of my old stories: "I always put things off until the last minute." This story, which took root early on in my school days (right around the time we started getting homework), eventually spread into many areas of my life. And instead of rewriting this pernicious little story, I reinforced it—telling it again and again and again. The story went something like this:

The Procrastinator

I'm a procrastinator. Always have been, always will be.

For my whole life, I've waited until the last possible minute to do things. I'm the guy at the mall, frantically buying presents on Christmas Eve. I'm the college student pulling an all-nighter to finish a term paper minutes before it's due. I'm the guy racing to get to the post office to mail my taxes on April 15 at 4:59 p.m.

Do I like being a procrastinator? No! It's stressful. It impairs my work. It deprives me of sleep. And it's not particularly great for my health. But that's just me. It's who I am. It's my M.O. It's how I roll.

I'm a procrastinator. Always have been, always will be.

~ The End ~

So, how do you like this story? Not very much? Me neither! But what's the big deal? A little old story can't hurt me, right?

Actually, that is *partially* right. A story like this wouldn't have seriously affected my life…if I'd just told it once or twice. But I didn't. I told it over and over again. I told it to friends, to family members, and to myself. And I did more than just tell it; I lived it. I got to know the story so well that I considered writing an entire book on this topic. I even had the perfect title: *Stop Procrastinating…Tomorrow!*

For a while, stories about procrastination weren't so bad. They made for entertaining conversation. Sometimes I'd get a good laugh out of them. Sometimes I could make them sound exciting. Sometimes both. ("So I finish my term paper in the nick of time, and I'm running across campus to turn it in before the five o'clock deadline, but I see my boss walking in front of me, which wouldn't have been a big deal except I'd called in sick that morning to give me time to finish the paper; so I dive behind a tree before he sees me, but I can't just hide out because by that time it's 4:52, so I crawl under a hedge, squirming through the mud on my belly until I finally…")

After enough repetitions, this story was no longer just a casual anecdote about a few isolated incidents—it was about a pattern, a way of life, an identity. The story came to define who I was (or at least who I thought I was, which can be just as significant). I was no longer just a guy who happened to procrastinate now and then—I had become "The Procrastinator" (which somehow sounds like a particularly bad Arnold Schwarzenegger movie—an *inaction* film, complete with unscintillating catch phrases such as, "I'll be back…when I get around to it").

Eventually, this story that had once seemed so harmless—or even amusing—began to show a sinister side. It spread well beyond its initial realm of taxes and term papers, and infected every area of my life with this overarching "master story":

I just barely make it—squeaking through just under the wire, just getting by but never really getting ahead, never getting on top of life. Yes, I accomplish what I absolutely need to (the bare minimum) but only under duress—when faced with tremendous stress and pressure. I can survive but not thrive.

This story wasn't particularly empowering (or fun) to begin with, and it got even worse as it morphed from a story about myself to a story about the world and life in general:

Life is hard. Life is a struggle. Just scraping by is incredibly stressful. That's just the way of the world—racing against the clock, putting out one fire after another. And as soon as you manage to put out one fire, the next one starts. It never ends.

Not surprisingly, retelling, reinforcing, and reliving this story eventually affected all aspects of my life:

- *Emotions* – I was chronically nervous, frazzled, and stressed.
- *Finances* – I was just getting by: hustling to scrape together rent by the first of every month, just barely covering basic necessities but never managing to save, get ahead, or build up the security of a nest egg.
- *Health* – I ended up with adrenal problems, fatigue, difficulty breathing, and a high risk for a host of other stress-induced health issues.
- *Family and Relationships* – I never had enough time to spend with loved ones because I was so busy racing from one urgent deadline to the next, putting out one fire after another. Even when I did make time for my wife and family, I was usually too stressed out (or exhausted from a just-made deadline) to be fully present.
- *Self-Esteem* – Retelling and identifying with such a negative story eroded my self-confidence and self-image. I started to see myself as just barely competent, certainly not a champion or a role model. Not someone I was proud to see in the mirror. Not the person I wanted to be.

Perhaps worst of all, I felt stuck in this story, as if there were no way out, no possibility for change, no hope that life could be any other way. I didn't want to live this story for another ten seconds, yet I could easily imagine living it for another ten years, twenty years, or for the rest of my life! Just the thought of this made me feel a giant pit in my stomach, but what could I do about it? After all, this was my life, not just a fictional story I'd written. I couldn't just "delete" this story and write a new one?

Or could I?

After all, I'd been practicing creative writing for decades. I'd spent years in grad school learning to write, edit, and fine-tune my stories until I got them just the way I wanted them to be. Why couldn't I apply the same approach to my real-life story? It was certainly worth a try. I had nothing to lose…except a bit of deadline-induced stress!

So I started the same way I would have with a fictional story: I looked at the story I already had ("I do things at the last possible moment"). Then I practiced some editorial discernment by separating the parts I wanted to keep from what I wanted to delete. In my procrastination story, I liked the "I do things" part, so I kept that, but I got rid of the stress-inducing part about "at the last possible moment." Next, I wrote a new story about who I am and how I live: comfortably on top of my life; successfully completing projects in a timely, relaxed manner; and feeling good about myself. And finally, unlike my grad-school creations, I had to actually *live* this new story.

And, lo and behold, I did!

The new story began to express itself in experiences and anecdotes such as "I finished my assignment a week ahead of time, got all my Christmas shopping done by early December, and filed my taxes in March." (As I write these words, in fact, it's March 14, and my wife and I just filed our taxes last week—more than a month ahead of the deadline!)

I realize that my new story may not have any more entertainment value or literary merit than "The Procrastinator," but it sure is a lot more fun (and relaxing) to live! The old story left me feeling stressed, trapped, and disempowered. This new one leaves me feeling lighter, stronger, more confident, and a whole lot happier, which is exactly the kind of life I want—for myself and for you!

What About You?

If this is the sort of change you also want for yourself, please know that it is possible! You don't have to spend your whole life stuck in an old story that's been holding you back, living patterns you don't enjoy, missing out on all that life has to offer. You can take back the power to create the life you want, reach your goals, and give your story the happy ending (and the happy *now*) you deserve!

And you can start immediately—by setting the intention to write and live a more empowering story. To claim your divine right to tell your own story the way you want to. To be the author of your own life rather than a character stuck in someone else's story (or a story you wrote years ago that no longer serves you). To take back your "pen" and your power.

Now, if you're feeling a bit skeptical—thinking that I'm making this whole process seem a bit *too* simple—you're right! As is usually the case for anything that looks too easy, there's more to it than meets the eye. Most seemingly simple stories (especially those involving significant change) have a lot going on behind the scenes and below the surface. And yes, it does take time, focus, and dedication. But rest assured, it *can* be done—you can rewrite even the most firmly entrenched story—and it may not be nearly as difficult or time-consuming as you think. If you apply yourself to the process described in this book, by the time you reach the end, you will have rewritten your story and redirected the course of your life.

Now *that* will be a happy ending!

But in order to make such a significant transformation, you've really got to want it—you've got to be motivated! So, let me ask you the all-important question…

What's Your Motivation?

Stories are about change. And in order to change, characters need a motivation—usually a pretty strong one. (Even then, characters tend to change reluctantly—often dragged from their known world against their will, kicking and screaming.) Without motivation, a character won't even get off the couch, much less embark on an epic transformational adventure!

In this sense, we real-life humans are a lot like our fictional counterparts—we need a pretty strong reason to interrupt our status-quo patterns, change the direction of our lives, and rewrite our story.

So, what's *your* motivation? Why would you want to make the effort to change your story? What part of your current life-story is causing you pain or dissatisfaction? What's the happy ending you're hoping to write (and live)? What would happen if you do (or don't) rewrite your story?

In short: *Why are you doing this?* Why are you bothering to read this book and go through this process? What's at stake?

Your motivation might be something physical (such as survival), emotional (such as love), or psychological/spiritual (such as self-esteem of self-actualization). You might be driven by a universal need, such as identity, stimulation, or security. Or you might have a very specific, personal motivation for changing.

For instance, I recently spoke with a young woman who said that if she didn't change the course she was on (her current "story") she would die— *literally* die—due to the stress it was causing and the toll it was taking on her body (illnesses that could be exacerbated by more stress). Wow! Now *that's* a motivation to change!

Your motivation for change doesn't have to be quite that dramatic, though. Perhaps you want to be healthy enough to play with your kids or grandkids. Or you want to run a half marathon to raise money for a charity that's near and dear to your heart. Or maybe you're just sick and tired of feeling sick and tired—and ready to feel great!

Of course, your story (the current one and the one you'd like to write/live) might not be focused on health. Maybe you feel stuck in a rut and you're ready to get out of it. Maybe you'd like to be more productive, efficient, and successful so that you can spend more quality time with your loved ones. Maybe you have creative urges that you want to express—to make sure that you don't "die with your music still inside you" (figuratively or literally). You might want to follow (and reach) your dreams in order to feel more personally fulfilled, share your gifts with the world, be a good role model for your kids, or all of the above. Maybe you have a very specific motivation, or maybe you just want to feel better in general—because feeling good is its own reward!

Regardless of what story you're changing—or are even *considering* changing—you need a compelling reason to change. What's yours?

What's your motivation?

Why are you reading this book? Why do you want to rewrite your story (even if you don't yet know what your story is—or have only a vague sense of it)?

What would happen if you don't rewrite your story?
If you keep telling/living the same old story you've been living, where would that lead you? (In other words, what's your "away-from" motivation—what negative scenario or experience would you like to avoid or move away from?)

What's your happy ending?
If you do rewrite your story and give it a best-case "storybook ending," what would that look like? (In other words, what's your "toward" motivation—that is, what positive scenario or experience would you like to move toward?)

How does it feel?
The #1 motivation for changing is to feel better—especially to feel better about yourself. With this in mind, ask yourself how you'd feel (in general and about yourself) if you don't change vs. if you do change.

So, do you have a pretty good idea of why you want to change your story, what might happen if you don't, and where you'd like your new story to lead? Even if you can't precisely put it into words yet, do you feel an inner urge—a strong motivation (or even a medium or small-but-growing motivation) to make a change in your life? If you do (and I assume you do since you're reading this book!), let's start the process of self-transformation.

So, how do you begin this process? As with almost any transformation, the first step is awareness. Before you can edit, revise, or rewrite your story, you have to know what your story is. That's why Part I of this book focuses on identifying your story—the one that's been controlling your life for far too long—so you can start taking back that control and taking back your life.

Other People's Stories: Looking Out, Looking In

Identifying your story requires a lot of introspection. It requires taking a good long look in the mirror and a clear-eyed, honest look at your life. It requires digging deep and also seeing what's right in front of your eyes. It requires self-focus.

Yet, throughout Part I and throughout this book, I frequently share other people's stories, and I also encourage you to consider the stories of people you know (or have heard about). This might seem odd for a book that's primarily about looking inward—examining your own life, identifying your own story, and creating something new that serves and reflects the person you want to be. Why devote any time at all to looking at other people's stories? There are several reasons:

- *To Provide Examples* – Adults tend to learn best when provided with specific examples rather than general principles. The case studies mentioned throughout this book (and the real-life stories of people you know) provide either role models of positive transformation or cautionary tales of pitfalls you hope to avoid.

- *To Eliminate Defensiveness* – When you identify someone else's story, there's no obligation to defend it or change it. So while you might be tempted to make excuses to justify your own story (and get out of the hard work of changing it), you can take a clear-eyed look at other people's stories without any onus to deal with its implications.

- *To Present Options* – Exploring the wide variety of other people's stories reminds you that your story isn't the only one available—that there are, as Cat Stevens sang, "a million ways to go."

- *To Highlight Similarities (and Differences)* – Looking at other people's stories can help you notice similarities with your own story. Or they can provide clarity through contrast—helping you gain insight about your own story by seeing how different it is from someone else's.

- *To Practice Noticing Stories* – As you get used to noticing other people's stories, this process will feel more natural, making it easier to notice your own story.

- *To Ease In* – Before diving into the deep end of your own story, you may find it more comfortable to wade through the shallow end of other people's stories (which, presumably, don't carry the emotional charge and high stakes that your own story does for you).

- *To Use the Creative-Writing Toolbox* – Since the RYS method is inspired by creative writing, we may as well use one of the most common tools of all fiction writers: drawing inspiration from the world around us. Many novelists and screenwriters base their characters on real-life people, and nearly all writers draw from situations and experiences in the world around them. Fiction isn't created in a vacuum, and neither is your life story. Why not learn from the examples of those around you?

But the main reason we'll explore other people's stories is because it's easier—for one simple reason: *Stories are written on your back.* They're like the signs that say "Kick Me" that mean kids used to tape on fellow students' backs (in the days before cyber-bullying). The idea was that everyone could see the sign…except for the kid who had it on their back!

It's the same with our stories. It's often easy to notice other people's stories but difficult to see your own. True, as an adult, the "sign on your back" may not say "Kick Me," but it might say "Poor Me" or "Look at Me" or "Love Me." (Although, if you have particularly low self-esteem and a particularly strong masochistic streak, maybe it *does* say "Kick Me"!)

So, how do you see the story/sign on your back? Perhaps a kind person can point it out for you. Or you might discover it through personal reflection—like seeing yourself in a mirror. Or you can train yourself to notice other people's stories and then look for possible connections with your own.

Aside from the aforementioned benefits of identifying other people's stories, this practice has the advantage of being extremely convenient—you can do it in almost any situation: when talking to a friend, overhearing snippets of conversations in public, reading social-media posts, or just thinking about the people in your life and seeing if you can identify their stories (some of which are fairly well hidden, others of which may be "hidden in plain sight").

One obvious story comes from someone I know who's always complaining about money. Whenever I ask how he's doing, he replies with his four-word (and one-grunt) story: "Ugh! I've got no money!" For some reason, this isn't charged for me, and I usually end up laughing to myself, thinking, "Who said anything about money? I just asked how you were doing!" The irony is that, despite his claims to the contrary, this guy is rather well off. But his story is so strong that it's become his reality, so it *is* "how he's doing"!

Stories don't have to come from someone you know in person—they could come from someone you've just heard of (such as a celebrity), a fictional character, or an online friend. For instance, I have a Facebook friend who starts nearly every post with something about how she's afraid to be seen. Even though she's supposedly transcending this story, she's actually reinforcing it more and more with each retelling—to the point where she's made it a central part of her identity.

Some people's stories may be long and complicated—tangled webs resulting from decades of experience. Other people's stories may be extremely short and simple—sometimes even just one word long. For instance, I know many people who, when asked how they are, invariably respond with their perennial one-word story: "Busy." (I've occasionally fallen into that story myself, which is certainly one I recommend rewriting!) And I know several people whose stories can be summarized by the word *but*. No matter what they're talking about or how good a situation seems to be, they always find a catch…and focus on it: "My boss unexpectedly gave everyone a paid day off this Friday, but that's just gonna make it harder to go back to work on Monday." "I made more money this year, but now I have to pay more taxes." "My boyfriend sent me flowers, but now I have to get a vase to put them in and somehow find a place for them in my house, which is already too cluttered." (Yes, that is an actual real-life example!)

Of course, not everyone's story is negative. In fact, some people's stories are the opposite of the *but* examples—no matter how challenging a situation is, they always find a silver lining. And some people have one-word stories such as *appreciation, curiosity*, or *love*.

So, how do you identify other people's stories (or your own)? First of all, remember that what's most important aren't the external events of someone's life as much as their perspective on those events—in other words, the story they tell based on their experiences. It's possible for people to describe similar situations in very different ways. For instance, if two people had a cold over the weekend, one of them might say:

"I came down with a bit of a cold, so I spent the weekend resting on the couch, watching funny movies, and reading a couple of books I've been wanting to read. It reminded me of

how important—and how nice—it is to relax. From now on, I'm going to make a point to rest and take care of myself…without needing to get sick! In any case, I'm feeling much better now."

The second person might describe a similar situation…but tell a very different story:

"My boss worked me extra hard all week, and then when I finally had a day off, I got sick…of course! And it just had to be on the nicest weekend of the year, so while everyone else was outside enjoying the sunshine, I was cooped up inside with a runny nose and a cough. And, sure enough, by the time Monday rolled around, all the symptoms were gone—so I couldn't even take a sick day from work. How typical of me and my stupid body!"

Same externals, very different stories, right?

I'd summarize the first person's story like this: *Things work out for the best. Even apparent setbacks contain valuable lessons, silver linings, and opportunities for growth and enjoyment.*

The second person's story is more along the lines of: *I'm a victim of people and circumstances beyond my control, I have the worst luck, and my life sucks.*

Sound pretty accurate?

One final reason to look for other people's stories is because you can learn a lot about yourself when you notice what you notice. If you habitually recognize the same type of story coming from many people, it might say more about *you* than about *them*!

In any case, you can usually gain tremendous insight, clarity, and objectivity from being able to stand back, view a person/situation from an emotional distance, and not be personally invested in their story. Maybe you'll want to incorporate elements of other people's stories into your own, or maybe you'll want to make sure you do the exact opposite. But at least it will remind you that you have choices.

Identify other people's stories

Before you start the process of identifying your own story, let's take some time to reflect on other people's stories. You can use total strangers, people you know well, or a bit of "thin-slice" information, such as their online posts. Pick three people and summarize their stories.

Person #1:
Story #1:

How do (or don't) you relate to Story #1? What insight might these similarities or differences provide into elements of your own story?

Person #2:
Story #2:

How do (or don't) you relate to Story #2? What insight might these similarities or differences provide into elements of your own story?

Person #3:
Story #3:

How do (or don't) you relate to Story #3? What insight might these similarities or differences provide into elements of your own story?

Some of the stories in this book are like snapshots—pictures of someone's life in that moment. However, the most important kinds of stories we'll examine are more like movies—stories that show transformation over time. These stories can serve as models for your own process, providing evidence that, yes, people do change—and that, no matter how deeply rooted a story may be, with a bit of reflection and conscious effort, you can rewrite it.

One example of a transformed story—one that took root in childhood and spread throughout adulthood…until it was consciously rewritten—comes from a woman we'll call "Karen" (She wished to remain anonymous, so we'll use this made-up name, chosen because she describes herself as a caring person—something she admits wasn't always true for her!) In addition to providing evidence that change is possible, Karen provides striking examples of how stories can be self-fulfilling prophecies—for better or worse!

Caring Karen: Self-Help Really Can Help!

As a child, Karen was told that she was dumb, plain, and a bad influence who would never amount to anything. Equally damaging were the stories she heard about other people and the world in general: for instance, that the people closest to her would hurt her the most.

As children tend to do, she took these messages to heart. Not only did she internalize them (through low self-esteem and low expectations of life), but they also manifested externally in many ways. She did poorly in school and was frequently bullied. As an adolescent, she ended up bullying others and also pushed people away with rudeness, mistrust, and aggression. As a young adult, she was a self-described "sarcastic, icy man-hater" who avoided intimate relationships, felt unlovable, went broke, suffered from depression, and even contemplated suicide.

Karen summarizes the underlying story of her early life as the "I'm not…enough" story (not good enough, pretty enough, intelligent enough, talented enough, qualified enough, confident enough, lovable enough, and so on). But rather than give in to these stories and give up on her life, she embarked on a path of self-help, including meditation, paraliminals (audio programs for relaxation and self-improvement), lots of reflection, and a steady diet of inspiring books by personal-growth authors such as Wayne Dyer, Deepak Chopra, and Louise Hay. And gradually, her stories began to change:

- "I'm dumb" became "I'm knowledgeable; and when I put in the effort, I learn and succeed."
- "I don't trust people" became "I trust that we meet people for a reason, whether as a lesson or a blessing."
- "My life is meaningless" became "I'm here for a reason."

- "I've made too many mistakes" became "My journey down the wrong paths can help people find the right ones."
- "I'm unlovable" became "I am loving, loved, and lovable."
- "I'm not enough" became "I am enough."

Although she admits that her life is still very much a work in progress, she says that she now feels appreciation for other people and the many blessings in her life, is able to support herself and others, and is depression free…and even sarcasm free (unless she was being sarcastic when she told me this)!

Don't Wait to Rewrite Your Story!

Even though Karen's core story was only three words long ("I'm not enough"), it took her years to identify it…and even longer to change it. And while I'm glad that she's rewritten this story, it pains me to think of all the years spent stewing in bitterness, self-loathing, and anger. It pains me to think of all the opportunities for love and connection that passed her by while she spun her wheels round and round in the same old self-defeating story. And it pains me even more to think of all the people who stay stuck in negative stories even longer than Karen did—or never rewrite their story at all—people who waste what could have been the best years of their life simply because they don't realize that they have the power to rewrite their story.

After reading several examples of stories—some that have been rewritten and some that haven't—you can see what a huge impact stories have on your life. And even if you're not yet sure what your own story is, you probably understand the consequences of rewriting it, not rewriting it, or (like Karen) wasting years of your life by spinning round and round in a story-rut.

Fortunately, with the help of this book, you don't have to wait years to change your story and your life. In fact, you don't have to wait another day! By the time you finish the first part of this book, you'll be able to identify your core story—and by the time you reach the end, you can already be living your new story.

But let's not get too far ahead of ourselves. Before you can rewrite a story, you have to know what that story is! And that's exactly what you're going to start discovering, piece by piece, in the next chapter.

CHAPTER TWO

The Elements of Story

Everyone tells a story about themselves inside their own head. Always. All the time. That story makes you what you are. We build ourselves out of that story.
— Patrick Rothfuss

NOW THAT YOU'VE LOOKED at several other people's stories, the time has come to ask: *What's YOUR story?*

This question may be more complex than it appears. You might think that because your story is such a big part of your life that it's incredibly obvious and easy to identify. But this isn't necessarily the case. Just like the old joke about the fish who doesn't know what water is, you may be so fully immersed in your story that you don't even recognize it.

You may have told your story so many times that you're not even aware when you do it—like an unconscious tic. You may see it as such a fixture of your life (like your height or your eye color) that you're not even aware that it can be changed. It may be a story your family (or social group or most of the world) has been telling since before you were even born. It may be the only story you've ever known—which makes it pretty hard to realize that it's just a story!

Regardless of how deeply ingrained or how widely shared your story may be, however, you can still become aware of it as just a story. But how do you do this? How do you identify the story you've been telling and living? The same way you put together a jigsaw puzzle: piece by piece.

As you piece together the puzzle of your story, you'll begin to see connections; and eventually, the whole picture will become clear. But before we get to that stage, the first step is to lay all the pieces out on the table—which is what we'll do in this chapter.

Taking Notes

As we'll do throughout this book, let's borrow the story-writing (or story-*discovery*) process used by most successful fiction writers. Writers don't generally have a single flash of insight during which their story is revealed in its entirety, complete with every last word and detail, as well as its implications and significance. (There are occasional exceptions, such as Samuel Coleridge "receiving" the entire poem "Kubla Khan" in a dream—but that was under fairly unusual circumstances.)

Most of the time, what happens is that an author has a starting point: a general idea, a theme they'd like to explore, an idea for a character, or a tiny detail (such as a sentence, an image, or a name). And then they take notes—writing down anything that might be related to the story, even if they have no idea if/how it all ties together. Finding connections is the next step; first, they simply write down possible "ingredients" for their story.

And that's the process we'll go through right now with your real-life story. You'll start by taking notes—jotting down possible storylines, character traits, bits of dialogue, scenes, and other elements that might (or might not) be part of your story.

Even if you've already got a pretty good idea of what your story's about, you might be able to uncover some hidden elements (which may be "hiding" in plain sight!) through this process. Or maybe you have no idea what your story is, but you'd like to find out.

Regardless of where you are in your story-writing/discovery process, let's consider some elements that can deepen your awareness and understanding of your story and your life.

But before you start writing—even if it's just jotting down a few notes (by hand or even making mental notes)—I'd like to make a suggestion, from one writer to another…

A Writer's Caveat: Blue Pen, Red Pen

Here's an important note about the note-taking process: *only use one pen at a time.*

I realize that this may sound like an odd suggestion. After all, if you're writing by hand, you *can't* use more than one pen at a time (unless you're ambidextrous and extremely talented). Yet many of us try to mentally "hold two pens at once" as we write. We try to write with a blue pen and a red pen at the same time, which is counter-productive, frustrating, and crazy-making.

Here's what it looks like for me: When I write notes or first drafts by hand, I usually use a blue pen. This is the playful pen—the pen that gets to create with childlike wonder, romping around the page without a care in the world for spelling, grammar, or even where I might be headed next. This is the pen I use for brainstorming, exploration, and creation.

During the next phase, when I edit, I use a red pen—marking up my first draft with deletions, insertions, and notes about what's working, what doesn't make sense, and how I might want to bring it all together in a cohesive way.

Both of these pens are valuable, but I can only hold one of them at any given time. When I get into trouble (and drive myself nuts) is when I let the "voice of the red pen" chime in while the blue pen is writing—saying things like, "That's not true" or "Don't write that; it's not important" or "Uh-oh…your family's not going to like reading *that*—maybe you'd better not write it in the first place. After all, if you don't have anything nice to say (or write)…"

It's not that the red pen's perspective isn't valuable—it is! Its role is vital. (If you don't believe me, try reading a self-published book that hasn't been edited!) It's just that this isn't its turn. The early stages of creation (brainstorming, taking notes, and writing a first draft) aren't the times for judging, editing, or censoring yourself. It's time for the blue pen. And the blue pen doesn't judge—it just writes.

So, as you go through the Part I exercises, remember that this is the blue pen's time, which means that you can explore the possibilities without worrying about whether or not they make sense, make a "good" story, or are even part of your story at all! All you have to do is stay open and write.

And if the red pen tries to butt in during the blue pen's time, you can reassure it that its time will come. It will be in charge while you sift through your notes, delete the parts you don't like, and build on the material that best serves the new story you want to write. When the time comes, the red pen will provide a crucial service. But that time hasn't come yet. And if you allow the red pen to have its way prematurely, you run the risk of censoring or pre-editing your words and stifling your story and your growth. And you probably won't get much of anything written.

So, as we move on to the exercises, let's pick up the blue pen (figuratively…and perhaps literally, too, if you plan on writing your answers) and consider all the possibilities for your emerging story—with an open mind and an open heart.

As you begin this process of examining the elements of your life that may or may not be part of your story, you're not only a writer—you'll also put on your detective's hat (again, figuratively…and perhaps literally, too, if you *really* want to get into the spirit). After all, right now, your story is a mystery, so we're going to look for clues that might reveal it…and help you crack your own case.

So, where do we start looking for clues? Let's follow the best piece of advice for almost any situation:

Start Where You Are

Before we go digging up the distant past or excavating the buried contents of your psyche, let's take a look at your life right now. How do you spend your days? What's your living situation? Are you in a relationship? What's the state of your health, finances, and other areas that are important to you?

As you look at your current reality, you'll probably find many clues about your story hiding in plain sight. For instance, if you're constantly struggling with money, work, health, and relationships, there's a good chance that your story is "Life is a struggle." If you constantly feel rushed—running behind schedule, running out of time, and saying (or even just thinking) things like "There just aren't enough hours in the day"—you might be living the story "There's never enough time" or just "There's never enough, period." If you spend most of your days taking care of your family, you're likely living a story that you derive your worth from personal connections, family, and your ability to give to others.

But for now, we don't have to jump ahead and try to discover (or analyze) your possible stories. Let's just start by taking an honest look at your current life situation.

Summarize Your Current Life

How do you spend your days? Where do you live, and who do you live with? What people and activities do you spend the most time with? What does a typical day look like for you?

Summarize Your Relationship(s) and Family

Do you have a significant other, or are you single? If you're in a relationship, describe it. If you're single, describe how that is for you (e.g., do you enjoy being single, or do you long for a relationship?). Do you live with your family (e.g., young children or aging parents)? If not, how big a role do they play in your current life?

Summarize Your Work

What do you do for a living? If you're currently employed, describe your work environment. If you're retired or don't currently work, describe that situation.

Summarize Your Finances

Do you have more than enough money for everything you want, enough to get by comfortably (but without much left over), just barely enough to scrape by, or not enough to get by? Are you in debt, or do you have a nest egg? How big a role does money play in your life (including your thoughts—e.g., is it a frequent source of worry, or do you rarely think about it at all)?

Summarize Your Health

Are you generally healthy, or do you suffer from frequent (or chronic) illness? Do you feel robust and full of vitality, sluggish and drained, or somewhere in between these extremes?

Summarize Other Aspects of Your Current Life

What other areas play a significant role in your daily life? Do you spend a lot of time on hobbies, leisure activities, creative pursuits, or spiritual practices? Aside from the areas mentioned above, how do you spend your time and what do you focus on?

Summarize Your Past

Although we're primarily focused on the present for now, take a few moments to reflect on where you've been. What have been your primary activities and areas of focus? What have been your predominant experiences in the areas mentioned above (relationships, family, work, money, and health)? How is your life now different from your past?

By reflecting on your current life (and taking a glimpse at your past), did you get any insight regarding what your story might be about? Even though we've just started the clue-gathering process, sometimes even a thin slice of life is enough to point you in the right direction.

However, even though the externals of your life may offer significant clues, they don't tell your entire story. Many other factors are involved, such as your thoughts and feelings about your external circumstances, as well as the stories you already tell about them. And that's what we'll look at next—not the big, overarching story but those small, seemingly casual anecdotes from your life that often serve as portals of insight and self-discovery.

Anecdotes

One of the main elements of any story is the scene—an incident, event, or anecdote that you might tell others. Not every anecdote is part of your larger story, however. There are two main differences between the two:

- *An anecdote is passing; a story is recurring.* Most anecdotes only get told once—or maybe a few times at most. They just aren't that significant (to the teller, at least). But a person's *story* gets told over and over and over because it's important to them.

- *An anecdote is casual; a story is charged.* It's usually easy to tell the difference just from someone's tone of voice. Are they just casually mentioning something they've experienced, or are they relating a situation that clearly presses their buttons or carries a lot of weight for them?

Depending on how (and how often) you tell it, the same scene could be either a simple anecdote or part of your bigger story.

For instance, if I get home from running some errands and casually mention to my wife that a man at the post office cut in front of me in line, that's probably just an anecdote. It doesn't feel charged, and I'd probably only mention it once. After that, I'd most likely let it drop and forget all about it.

If, however, I related the incident in an angry voice—cursing that "jerk" who had the nerve to cut in front of me, thinking that his time is more important than mine (etc., etc., etc.)—there's a good chance that this would-be anecdote is an element of (or a clue about) my bigger story. Especially if I repeat this story to others. And doubly so if I'm still stewing over it hours (or days, months, or years) later.

In the second scenario, this experience has clearly pushed one of my buttons, indicating that it's probably part of a bigger story. (After all, for someone or something to push your button, the button's got to be there in the first place.) What exactly that story is remains to be determined. Maybe the story is that people are always taking advantage of me (or taking advantage of others in general). Or that men are rude. Or that it's a cutthroat world in which people do anything to get ahead.

Most likely, the emphasized details provide clues about the story's significance to you: Maybe it's that rich people are inconsiderate (if I mentioned the man's expensive suit). Or that I feel invisible (if I say that the man cut right in front without even noticing me). Or that I never speak up until it's too late (if I didn't say anything at the time…but wished I had). Or that technology is ruining the world (if I mention that the line-cutter was too wrapped up in texting on his cell phone to even notice what he was doing).

Later on we'll consider what the story behind your anecdotes might be. First, however, take some time to write down the anecdotes you tell (or even think about) and consider which ones might be part of your bigger story.

Your Anecdotes
What are some anecdotes you've told?

Inner Anecdotes
What are some anecdotes or scenes that you've returned to in your thoughts—long after the actual incident?

Do you repeat it?
Of the anecdotes you mentioned above (or any others that you can think of), which ones do you tell most often—especially when you're just meeting and getting to know someone?

Is it charged?

When you tell these anecdotes (or stories) do you get worked up? Does your voice get louder or change in tone? Are you able to let it go quickly, or do you stew in the story? Does it carry more weight, significance, or meaning than a typical everyday experience? Does it press your buttons? Write down the anecdotes from above (or any others you can think of) that might fall into the "story" category—and describe their charge for you.

Is it a significant part of you?

What stories are so integral to your identity that if someone didn't know them, you don't feel that they would really know you? How do these stories define or embody your identity?

Patterns: Recurring Themes and Motifs

As you look at your current life and reflect on your past, the biggest clues about your story probably aren't the one-time experiences, minor details, or anecdotes mentioned casually in passing and then forgotten. The key story in your life probably relates to the anecdotes you tell and the experiences you have over and over again. What elements of your life seem to keep popping up again and again? For instance, do you always seem to date controlling partners? Have you spent years just scraping by financially? Have you shied away from opportunities that you really wanted because you didn't think you deserved them?

Remember that when identifying elements that might be part of your story, you're looking not only for recurring externals (e.g., frequently talking about writing), but also for recurring themes (e.g., frequently talking about struggle). You're looking for the stories you repeat (although possibly in different forms), the ones you live, the ones that define you.

Take some time right now to reflect on your frequently told anecdotes, habitual thoughts/emotions, and recurring experiences and look for the patterns and themes.

(Note: You may want to do this with a friend, a partner, or a counselor or therapist—or by looking back over old journals. If you'd like to, you can summarize the story of your life, either out loud [to another person or into a recording device] or written in a journal.)

Don't worry—I'm not asking you to retell your entire life story or to write a full-length autobiography. Just like a novelist wouldn't describe every single detail about a character and their situation, you're not going to recount every part of your entire life —you're just focusing on the telling details, the recurring stories, and the defining moments. Remember, you're not just looking for *what happened*, you're looking for your story.

I hope you'll take some time right now to identify the recurring themes that reveal important aspects of your character and your story. Before you begin this process, however, I'd like to offer these two caveats:

- While self-reflection is incredibly valuable, be aware that your story might be so close that it's hard to spot in yourself. It's like having a word written on your forehead—unseen by you but easy for others to notice. Other people (or even your old journals/diaries) can serve as mirrors.

- If you're discussing your life with a partner, friend, or family member, please encourage them to be honest and not sugarcoat any patterns or stories they may notice you telling/living. The point of this exercise isn't to protect your ego but to increase your awareness, so please enter it with an open heart, an open mind, and a spirit of growth. Their honesty can be the catalyst for tremendously positive shifts in your life—but only if you're open to it.

After you've taken some time to reflect on your life (alone, with another person, or with your journals), answer the following questions:

What patterns did you notice?

Or, if you were talking with another person, what patterns did *they* notice? Ask them—and be open to their honest impressions.

What are your recurring external themes?

Do you have a type of romantic partner you've tended to get involved with— or other predictable relationship patterns? Do you generally take risks or play it safe? Have you repeatedly sabotaged yourself when you were right on the brink of a breakthrough? Do any other types of situations or people make frequent appearances in your life story?

What are your emotional patterns?

For instance, do you frequently feel depressed, angry, nervous, happy, excited, or any other emotion?

What are your recurring thoughts or "mental loops"?

For instance, are you constantly beating yourself up about not finishing a creative project, worrying about money, second-guessing whether or not you're on the right career path or in the right relationship, feeling like an outsider who doesn't fit in with others, or mentally replaying past incidents?

Are you starting to get a sense of your personal story?

What story elements or motifs—such as key words, phrases, or images—are emerging?

By this point, you might feel that you've already identified your full story. If so, fantastic! You've taken a huge, important step in this transformational process.

But not all stories are so easy to discover. It may take a little more sleuthing to identify yours. Or maybe you're beginning to get a sense of your story, but you'd still like to uncover some of its hidden elements. (After all, there's usually much more to a story than meets the eye—just like there's more to *you* than meets the eye.)

Regardless of where you are in your story-discovery process, you can certainly learn more about your story and yourself by examining your subtext—in other words, "reading between the lines."

Subtext: Reading Between the Lines

One of the cardinal sins of fiction writing is "on-the-nose" dialogue. It's a hallmark of bad writing. Once you become aware of it, it sticks out like a sore thumb (or a cliché).

"On the nose" means that characters say exactly what they're thinking—no hidden agenda, no ulterior motive, no mystery, no dissembling, no denial, no subtext. Anne is happy, so she says, "I'm happy." Bobby loves her, so he says, "I love you, Anne." And she says (completely without guile), "I love you, too, Bobby." (Another hallmark of bad dialogue, by the way, is characters calling one another by name. In real one-on-one conversations, this rarely happens.)

One reason why on-the-nose dialogue is so bad (in fiction) is that it leaves no room for mystery, subtlety, or interpretation. It also insults the reader's intelligence. (We readers tend to be more adept at picking up on subtlety and nuance than many hack writers give us credit for; we can generally get the author's point without being hit over the head with it.) Plus, it simply isn't realistic: actual people don't generally say exactly what they're thinking—completely honestly, transparently, and without any subtext. (Yes, it might be nice if they did—so you wouldn't have to play guessing games or hire a detective to figure out what someone is actually thinking or feeling.) Or they might only tell you what's true on the surface of things without unpeeling the outer layer to reveal what's *really* going on. (For instance, a married couple's argument about the towels probably isn't really about the towels—it's about how one of them is inconsiderate about the other's feelings…or any number of other deeper issues.)

Yes, some people come right out and express their thoughts in an honest, forthright, and on-the-nose way. More often than not, however, there's an underlying message (that the speaker might not even be conscious of) encoded in their words that you figure out by reading between the lines—or, if it isn't written, by picking up on nonverbal cues such as tone of voice. (For instance, think of someone saying, "I'm FINE!" in an angry voice.)

Subtext isn't just relevant in fictional stories—it's a key element of our real lives and the stories we tell every day. For instance, I probably wouldn't come right out and tell someone, "I'm a procrastinator—a characteristic trait that informs my self-image and extends to my entire worldview, leading to me to believe that just scraping by is a stressful struggle."

But I might say, "Whew! Once again, I filed my taxes minutes before the deadline! I thought I was gonna have a heart attack racing to the post office!" I might say this with a self-flagellating tone or perhaps with a touch of pride. Or I might take a sarcastic tone of voice when saying something like, "I think I'll finish my project well ahead of the deadline…yeah, right!"

If someone heard me repeatedly relate anecdotes and make comments such as these, it probably wouldn't be too hard for them to read between the lines and pick up on the (not-so-subtle) subtext.

Are you able to read between the lines of your own stories? Can you identify your own subtext?

What's the subtext of the stories you commonly tell (and live)?
Review the anecdotes you wrote down earlier (or any others that come to mind), and ask yourself: What am I *really* saying when I tell these stories? What's going on under the surface or "between the lines"?

Messages and Morals: What's Your Point?

You can also think of subtext in terms of a story's message or moral—not in the sense of ethics and morality, but in terms of the point being conveyed. For instance, think of the famous morals in Aesop's Fables:

- "The Tortoise and the Hare" – Slow and steady wins the race.
- "The Fox and the Goat" – Look before you leap.
- "The Four Oxen and the Lion" – United we stand, divided we fall.
- "The Fox and the Grapes" – It is easy to despise what you cannot get (the origin of the expression "sour grapes").

True, these aren't the sort of morals that generally appear in literary fiction. While they're appropriate in parables (as well as in self-help books, motivational blogs, and other personal-growth writing), such overt messages can turn would-be literary fiction into two-dimensional propaganda (a cardinal sin even worse than on-the-nose dialogue).

Most fiction writers (and readers and critics) recoil at the thought of using a story as a thinly veiled contrivance for sending a message. In fact, an oft-cited dictum among writers is that "If you want to send a message, use Western Union" (an extremely outdated reference—these days you might say, "If you want to send a message, just text me"—but, in either form, it gets the point across).

Another issue with overt morals is that, as with on-the-nose dialogue, they simply aren't realistic. In everyday life, people don't generally spew messages or morals on one another. Overt messages are usually reserved for speeches, sermons, or other "soapbox" platforms.

This doesn't mean, however, that messages aren't being conveyed. They are—constantly—by those around you and by yourself. You may not even be aware of the messages you're sending—the "moral" of your story, as it were— but you can discover it by reading between the lines, examining clues and cues (including nonverbal cues), and also by looking for recurring themes.

For instance, if I'm telling an anecdote from the "Procrastinator" series— something about how waiting until the last minute made me stressed out, lowered the quality of my work, and possibly cost me money (or, if it's a term paper, a letter grade or two)—then the moral of my story might be: "Plan ahead" (or, to phrase it as a double negative, "Don't wait until the last minute").

For my old story about not finishing/publishing my books, the moral might be: "Don't die with your music in you."

When you tell (or reflect on) your own most commonly recurring anecdotes, ask yourself: *Why am I telling this? What message do I want to convey? What's my point?* If you can answer this, you may have just found the moral of your own story.

If your anecdotes/stories had a moral (like one of Aesop's Fables), what might it be?
In other words, what's the point of the stories you retell most often?

What's Your Catch Phrase?

Sometimes a moral, message, or recurring theme is fairly easy to spot. Other times it's subtle or hidden and might take some careful examination or further reflection to discover. Occasionally, however, people will come right out and say it—spelling it out for you in no uncertain terms with a catch phrase that summarizes their attitude, plight, or character.

Catch phrases are a staple of cartoons (e.g., Homer Simpson's annoyed grunt: "D'oh!"), books (Sherlock Holmes: "Elementary, my dear Watson"), comedy skits (Dana Carvey's "Church Lady" character on SNL: "Well, isn't that special"), and song lyrics (most hit songs ever written). In fact, it's been shown that the more often a song repeats its title phrase, the more likely it is to be a hit. For an example of a musical catch phrase, consider the following lyrics (by Tom Adair—although you might recognize the words from renditions by Billie Holiday, Ella Fitzgerald, Frank Sinatra, or others):

> *I make a date for golf and you can bet your life it rains.*
> *I try to give a party and the guy upstairs complains.*
> *I guess I'll go through life just catchin' colds and missin' trains.*

In case you missed the not-so-subtle message, it's stated directly in the following line (which is also the song's catch phrase and title): "Everything Happens to Me."

Catch phrases can also be used for comic effect. For instance, have you ever seen Rodney Dangerfield's old stand-up comedy bits where he used the catch phrase, "I don't get no respect"? In case you missed the routine, here are a few of his classic self-deprecating jokes:

- When I was born, the doctor came out to the waiting room and said to my father, "I'm very sorry. We did everything we could…but he pulled through."
- They wanted to make me a poster boy…for birth control.
- I went to see my doctor…I told him, "Doctor, every morning when I get up and look in the mirror, I feel like throwing up. What's wrong with me?" He said, "I don't know, but your eyesight is perfect."
- My psychiatrist told me I'm going crazy. I told him, "If you don't mind, I'd like a second opinion." He said, "All right. You're ugly too!"
- A girl phoned me and said, "Come on over. There's nobody home." I went over. Nobody was home!

Even if you didn't know Rodney's catch phrase, you'd probably get the point, right? Although his routine had countless variations, the jokes all revolved one central theme: He gets no respect! That was his schtick—the recurring theme of his mini-stories.

Catch phrases can make for memorable songs and funny comedy routines, but they can also show up in our everyday lives. Although people often convey their story in subtext and subtlety, sometimes they spell it right out for you with a signature catch phrase. Do you know anyone who has an oft-repeated catch phrase, or do you have your own? Perhaps something like:

- I'm swamped!
- I wasn't born with a silver spoon in my mouth!
- All the guys I date are such jerks.
- Just my luck!
- I can't hold on to money—as soon as I get a bit, it starts burning a hole in my pocket.

- Things have been kind of crazy lately.
- I'm not happy unless I have something to complain about.

(I actually heard a guy use that last one recently, and I nearly fell off my chair! Can you imagine the implications this phrase/attitude must have on his life?)

Or perhaps you have a more positive catch phrase, such as:

- I am truly blessed.
- Aren't my kids just the best?
- I live a charmed life.
- Isn't that wonderful?
- Woo-hoo!

Or your catch phrase might convey a worldview (which can be positive or negative), such as:

- Everything happens for a reason.
- God helps those who help themselves.
- Give 'em an inch, they'll take a mile.
- What goes around comes around.
- There's always a catch.
- *C'est la vie!*

…or any other phrase you find yourself saying (or implying) on a regular basis.

Take a moment now and see if you can identify one or more phrases that might be your catch phrase—and probably a piece of your story.

If you had a catch phrase, what would it be?
Would it be "Everything happens to me," "I don't get no respect," another one of the above examples, or something entirely different?

The Missing Piece

By this point, you've identified enough of your story's elements that you're probably getting a pretty good sense of what that story is. It's almost like you're putting together a puzzle and you've got most of the pieces laid out in front of you. Or like being a chef who's just laid out most of the ingredients necessary to cook a meal. But there's still one missing piece—one key ingredient—that's at the center of your story.

Yes, you've explored the stories you tell, how you tell them, and the possible messages they convey. But it's important to remember that every story needs a character—and your protagonist, the character at the heart of your story, is *you*!

In the next chapter, you'll take a good look at your story's main character—inside, outside, and all around—and see how you affect your story...and how your story affects *you*.

CHAPTER THREE

Your Character, Your World

The universe is made of stories, not of atoms.
— Muriel Rukeyser

SOME WRITERS SAY that character creates story. And it's easy to see why they make this assertion. After all, whether you're looking at fiction or real life, the person at the center of the action plays a big role in how things turn out.

But other writers say it's the other way around: story shapes character. In other words, they claim that it's the situations someone goes through—and how they respond to those situations—that determine the kind of person they become.

Either way you look at it, story and character definitely affect each other, and the main character is an essential part of *any* story. Change one and you change the other as well.

For instance, imagine a pacifist playing the lead role in *The Godfather, Die Hard*, or *Rambo*. They certainly would have had to come up with alternate methods for dealing with the challenges they faced…or quit being a pacifist!

Or, to take a real-life example, consider a different person in Mahatma Gandhi's situation. Someone else might have submitted passively, shied away from controversy or confrontation, or responded with violence. What a different story these "characters" would have created!

As you consider your story, remember the crucial character at the heart of all your stories: your "protagonist"—in other words, you.

A Character Sketch...of Yourself

Good authors need to know a lot about the character at the center of their stories. Some authors keep files of character notes. Others fill out a character résumé. And some write character sketches (short scenes or descriptions) or conduct character interviews—full of questions and answers not intended to go directly in their books but merely to get to know their characters better.

You can do the same with yourself: sketch a picture of your "character" by asking yourself questions about your own defining characteristics, your worldview, and the significant experiences that have molded your character and shaped your story.

Imagine that you are the main character in your life's story (which you are) and describe the following details about this character (drawing on the insights you've gleaned while completing the previous exercises—or anything else you know about your character):

Most Noticeable Qualities

Which of your character's qualities are most clearly evident to others (e.g., kind, creative, belligerent, quirky, shy, charming, funny, confident)?

Less Noticeable Significant Qualities

What qualities are *not* obvious to most others but still play a significant part in your character's experience (e.g., insecure, reflective, full of repressed anger, or other qualities that aren't generally expressed outwardly)?

Skills/Talents/Proclivities

What is your character particularly good at? What do they particularly enjoy?

Obstacles/Challenges

What challenges does your character face (or have they faced in the past)? How have they responded? How have these challenges shaped their character—and what do their responses reveal about their character?

Secret Fear

What concerns keep your character up at night—or worrying in the middle of the day?

Secret Hope

What does your character wish for most deeply in their heart of hearts?

Character Under Stress

How does your character respond to stressful situations? How is this different from how they normally are?

Character in Comfort
How does your character act (and feel) when they are extremely comfortable? How is this different from how they are in other situations?

Attitude
How would you summarize your character's general attitude toward life (e.g., relaxed, uptight, cynical, optimistic)?

Worldview/Philosophy
How would your character complete the sentence, "The world is..." (e.g., good, random, meaningless, cold, empty, loving, divine)?

Self-Image
How does your character view him- or herself? What do they think about their appearance, age, intelligence, abilities, accomplishments, or other major aspects of their life—or about themselves in general (e.g., "I'm a pathetic, middle-aged underachiever, and my nose is too big" or "I'm an attractive, intelligent, and competent person with many important accomplishments under my belt that make me feel proud")?

Labels

What are some labels your character gives him- or herself—or that have been given by others (e.g., procrastinator, victim, survivor, dreamer, underachiever, "the pretty one," "hopeless romantic," or any other defining words/phrases)?

Obsession

Does your character have an obsession—something that occupies (or preoccupies) a large amount of their time, energy, thoughts, attention, and actions? If not, what's the closest thing they *do* have to an obsession?

Values

What's most important to your character?

Beliefs

What does your character believe about life, religion, and people (including themselves)?

Upbringing

How was your character raised? What was their childhood like? How did this affect the adult they became?

Other Notable Qualities and Characteristics

What other factors play a significant role in shaping your character (e.g., physical qualities/limitations, personal tastes and aesthetics, gender, sexual orientation)?

Character Arc

Your answers to the previous questions might provide a good snapshot of your character. But it's still only a snapshot—namely, a static picture of an ever-changing person. But your life is less like a snapshot and more like a movie: You *move*. You go places. You take action. You change.

Likewise, in most great stories, characters aren't static—they grow, evolve, and experience what's usually referred to as a "character arc." This might mean that they move from innocence to experience, from weakness to strength, or from insecurity to confidence, or that they make some other major shift in how they interact with their world.

As you engage with this book's material, you're most likely going to experience a dramatic character arc—and you will get to decide exactly what you want that to entail. (Remember, you're not a passive character, subject to an author's whims—you are both the character and the author of your own story.)

You might strengthen character "muscles" and talents that had been long neglected. You might develop characteristics that had previously been overlooked. Or you might take an unexpected turn and end up pursuing areas of yourself that you'd never even considered.

But the experience of a character arc is not new for you. You've been developing your character your entire life—and will continue to do so for as long as you live.

To give yourself a better understanding of yourself and a fuller picture of your character, consider how you've changed and evolved so far—and consider ways in which you might (or might *like to*) change in the near future.

Your Character Arc, Part 1: Changes So Far

How has your character evolved over time throughout their life? What major (or subtle) shifts have they already experienced? How are they different now than they were a year ago? Ten years ago? Twenty years ago? As a child? How would you summarize their character arc so far?

Defining Moments, Defining Choices

What experience(s) most deeply affected your character and shaped their attitudes, beliefs, and outlook? What choices did they make at that moment—or afterward, as a result of it—that dramatically shifted the course of their life? (Keep in mind that, despite its name, a character arc is not always a smooth, steady curve; frequently, it's more realistically represented by straight lines that occasionally veer off in a very different direction—often as a result of significant choices or other major life events.)

Your Character Arc, Part 2: Possibilities

What would you like your character arc to look like from this point on? What are some ways in which you might like your character to change in the near future? The mid-range future? The distant future? (You're not committing to making any changes right now—just considering some possibilities.)

Supporting Cast of Characters

You are not just yourself. You are a composite of every person who ever influenced you in any way. This includes those who played a major role in your life (such as parents, siblings, best friends, and significant others) as well as those who may have been part of your life briefly but who nonetheless left an indelible mark upon you (such as an exceptional teacher, an author whose book touched you deeply, or even a complete stranger whose passing remark changed the course of your life).

No story consists of a single person. Even a one-man or one-woman show always incorporates stories about the people who touched the storyteller's life. (Even if the storyteller doesn't overtly mention a single other person, they wouldn't be the way they are, telling/living the story they are, without the influence of other people.) Likewise, your life story isn't just about you, the protagonist. It involves a huge supporting cast of everyone who's ever helped to mold your character and set you on the path you're on today.

Take some time now to reflect on the "characters" in your life who've had the biggest impact on you.

Major Characters

Who's had the biggest impact on your life (in positive or negative ways)? What people have been the most significant presence in your life—externally (such as a parent or spouse) and internally (the people whose voices you most often hear in your head...even when they're not around)?

Small But Significant Roles

What people have you not known that well but who nonetheless had a major effect on the person you've become? (For instance, it might have been a boss who mentored you for a short but significant time, or perhaps even a complete stranger on a street corner or subway car who handed you a leaflet that opened you up to a new spiritual path.)

I hope you've enjoyed reflecting on who you are now, who you've been in the past, and who you may become in the future—and that you've gained insight into the lead character of your life's story…as well as some of the supporting characters who've helped you become who you are. We've certainly covered a lot of ground already, but we still haven't encompassed every aspect of your story. In addition to plot and character, there's still one more major element that goes into any story…

Your Story's World

If you're telling a story—in a novel, in a screenplay, or out loud to friends—one of the first things you'll mention is the setting. In other words, you'll answer the question, "Where is this taking place?" And the answers to that question are literally infinite. A story might take place halfway around the globe, "somewhere over the rainbow," inside a computer, or "in a galaxy far, far away." It might be set in present time, in the near future, or in the distant past. It might be set in a world of magic (like the Harry Potter series), a world of suburban alienation (like the stories of John Cheever), or a world of absurdity (like the works of Franz Kafka).

A story's world also includes the society that it focuses on: middle-class suburbanites, high society, or underworld thugs. And every world contains its own set of rules: You get three (and only three) wishes. If you want to remain safe, stay on the Yellow Brick Road. You don't talk about Fight Club. You do what the boss says…or else.

Even when a story involves magic, science fiction, or supernatural touches, the rules have to remain internally consistent—for instance:

- In *Groundhog Day*, every day starts exactly the same way—until you learn life's most important lesson.
- Superman is *always* allergic to kryptonite—not just some of the time.
- In Kafka's "Metamorphosis," Gregor Samsa is always an insect—he can't change back into a human at will.

Even if your world seems relatively commonplace (compared to, say, the Harry Potter books), there are still rules that govern its existence. They might be beliefs, societal norms, or conditions that your family taught you. They might be assumptions about people or the world in general—ideas that you simply take for granted.

Rules often show up in the form of if-then statements that you accept (perhaps unquestioningly) or any other statement that you assume is a given condition of your world. For instance, some rules of your world might be:

- If you want to succeed, then you've got to go to college.
- If you want to succeed, then you've got to struggle and sacrifice.
- If you want to keep your friends and romantic partners, then you can't express your anger.
- If someone's rich, they must be greedy.
- It's selfish not to have kids.
- Real men always provide for their family.
- Real men make an honest living through manual labor.
- Real men always keep it together—they keep their emotions on the inside.
- If he loved me, he would change.
- Relationships are hard work.
- The most valuable things in life are the hardest to attain.

...or any other statement you assume to be true about the world.

Although your rules may seem immutable, many of them are entirely subjective, self-created, or even arbitrary.

In other words—they aren't necessarily Rules of the Universe but simply rules of *your* universe. Which means that by changing the rules, you can literally change not just your story or your character but your *entire world*!

Take some time to examine your story's world—complete with its setting, rules, and other characteristics—and how this world affects your story and your lead character.

In what world does your story take place?

Describe your story's setting—including location, social circles, atmosphere, or other conditions that characterize the world in which your character lives.

What are the "rules" of this world?

What are the "if-then" conditions, assumptions, or other rules of this world? Which of them could be changed (in other words, aren't necessarily true for everyone all the time)?

What is the relationship between your character and their world?

How is your character affected by their world (including location, living situation, and the rules of their social scene)? How have they been shaped by their environment (present and past, including where they grew up)? Does their current environment reflect them? Which aspects of their world does your character embrace and which ones do they reject? What does this reveal about your character?

Weaving the Threads Together

You've now uncovered and explored all the elements that make up a great story. You've looked at your story's Who, What, and Where (your character, your arc, and your story's world), as well as numerous other elements, such as scenes (anecdotes), dialogue (catch phrases), and backstory (relevant information about your past). You've filled out your story with a supporting cast of characters, including family, friends, romantic partners, and other significant relationships. You've even looked at your story with a literary eye, reflecting on its recurring themes, subtext, and perhaps even a moral or message. And you've taken plenty of notes about details that flesh out a three-dimensional character, such as work, money, health, and hopes and plans.

I hope that taking all these notes and identifying your story's elements has been an enjoyable and eye-opening process for you and that you've gained a lot of clarity as you've reflected on key areas of your life. But no matter how many elements of your story you've looked at, you still haven't revealed your *story*. To do that, you have to take all these pieces and figure out how they fit together...which is exactly what we'll do in the next chapter.

CHAPTER FOUR

Your First Draft

To live is to write a story. If you are a strong person, your life story will mostly be written by you; if you are a weak person, mostly others will write your life story!
— Mehmet Murat ildan

THE TIME HAS COME to take all the threads you've identified and weave them together into a first draft of your story. Just like the first draft of a fictional short story or novel, you'll have a chance to edit and shape the story to match your ideal version. This is just a starting point, so there's no pressure to "get it right." (Keep in mind James Thurber's words, "Don't get it right, just get it written"—a perfect motto for authors working on their first draft.)

So, let's take the first steps to "get it written" by reviewing the elements you've explored in the last few chapters and adding anything new that might emerge right now. Then we'll figure out how it all fits together. For now, start by summarizing the following elements of your story (very briefly—using only a short sentence, a phrase, or even just a single word for each element).

Current External Reality

What does your life currently look like in terms of relationships, living situation, work, finances, health, and other significant areas?

Anecdotes

Summarize the anecdotes that you tell most often or that carry the most charge.

Recurring Themes

Summarize the themes of these anecdotes or other oft-repeated stories/experiences.

Subtext/Message

What is the subtext or message of your stories? In other words, what's your point? What are you *really* saying?

Catch Phrase

If you had a catch phrase, what would it be? (This could be anything you often say or even just think, such as "Everyone's struggling these days," "I'm too old for this," or "Just my luck!")

Other People's Stories

After reflecting on other people's stories, how would you summarize the one that stuck out the most? How does (or doesn't) it relate to your own story?
Person:
Their Story:

Relation to Your Story:

Labels

What single words or short phrases do you apply to yourself? Write down as many as you can think of (e.g., artist, procrastinator, overachiever, underachiever, workaholic, martyr, rock, super mom, family man, lone wolf, happy-go-lucky) and then circle the one that's most fitting.

Character

How would you summarize your "character" (as if you were the protagonist in a book or film) in a single sentence?

Character Arc

How would you summarize your character arc (the shifts in your personality and/or how you relate to the world—in other words, how you've changed over the course of your life)?

Your World

How would you describe the world you inhabit (your environment/milieu and the people you most often associate with)?

Rules

What are the rules that govern this world (the if-thens, the dos and don'ts, and other assumptions)?

Common Threads: Looking for the Master Story

Now that you've taken some time to answer and review the previous questions, you're probably getting a good grasp of your story's elements. You've done the equivalent of a novelist writing all their notes—brainstorming for themes and ideas, anecdotes and scenes, character and setting. You've got the pieces of your story. Now it's time to figure out how they all fit together.

And we want to make sure that these pieces really do fit—that they aren't random elements that have nothing to do with one another or with your story as a whole. To put it in fiction-writing terms, we want to make sure that your story is cohesive rather than episodic.

A major complaint that's leveled against many unsuccessful novels or screenplays is that they're episodic. That is, the individual scenes aren't woven together. There's no "spine" to hang them on. It's like a TV show where the episodes from one week to the next don't have anything to do with one another.

(The surefire test for whether or not a story is episodic is to ask: If any of the scenes are removed, would it work on its own? Would the rest of the story still work without the removed scene? Do all the pieces hang together? Is there a clear cause-and-effect from one scene to the next? If a story's *not* episodic, removing any single scene should make the story lose its impact, not make as much sense, or even fall apart altogether. In fiction, this is a good sign—it means that your story is cohesive.)

Being episodic is fine in some types of writing, such as short-story collections, picaresque novels (such as *Don Quixote*), or comedy-skit TV shows (especially if it's done intentionally, as Monty Python used to do blatantly with their between-sketch announcements: "...and now for something completely different!"). But your life is not a series of random moments, disconnected scenes, or unrelated episodes. Your life is a cohesive unit of interconnected elements that build on one another, tied together by common threads.

So, what are those common threads of your emerging story? What are the elements that make your life a cohesive story rather than an episodic collection of disconnected, random moments?

As practice, let's look at someone else's story elements and see if we can identify the common thread—imagining that they had the following experiences:

- They start a new relationship, everything's going great, and then they panic and break it off—or do something that almost guarantees that their partner will break up with them.

- They start a new job, everything's going great, they're about to get a desirable promotion, but then they suddenly quit—or do something that almost guarantees they'll get fired.

- They stick to a diet, make it 90% of the way to their ideal weight, but then fall off the wagon and gain it all back—and then some.

- Their catch phrase is, "So close, but yet so far."

- They refer to themselves as "Mr. Almost" or "Ms. Almost."

What do you think is the common thread here? I'd say that these elements are all tied together by the common theme of self-sabotage (particularly following strong starts). They might summarize their story by saying, "Just when I'm about to reach my goal, something goes wrong" (or, if they're willing to take responsibility for their life, "Just when I'm about to reach my goal, I find a way to mess it up").

As you look for your own "master story"—the underlying principle that connects your thoughts, beliefs, actions, emotions, and experiences—

remember that the events of your life aren't isolated incidents. The episodes aren't episodic. They're all tied together by *something*.

So, when you reflect on the various episodes of your life—as well as the other story elements you've written about—ask yourself how they're related. What's the connection? What common threads can you identify?

Common Threads

What ties together the significant elements of your life story (including those you summarized above: anecdotes, labels, character arc, etc.)? What do most (or all) of them have in common?

Subplots

But what about the pieces that don't seem to fit in with the others but are still significant parts of your life? Should you ignore those pieces? Not necessarily. These are frequently the parts of your life that add depth to your character and your story. While they might not be part of your main story, they can still be important subplots that you can embrace, celebrate, and weave into your life in meaningful ways.

The same thing is true in movies, novels, TV series, and other works of long-form fiction: they don't generally just have one big story and that's it; they have at least one subplot. An intense TV drama might have a humorous subplot. A romance novel might have a subplot centered around the lead character's friends, family, or job. And action movies frequently have a romantic subplot. (In fact, most movies have a romantic subplot.)

Subplots often reinforce the main plot—although they might run counter to it in order to explore the complexity of the story, the characters, and life in general. Subplots can reveal different aspects of the protagonist's personality. Or they might just lighten the mood of an otherwise serious drama.

Like good, rich fiction, your own life also has subplots. So far in this book, we've focused primarily on your main plot—the Big Picture or "A" story of your life—but there's clearly much more to you. You're not just a two-dimensional character. You have many sides, many experiences, and many stories—major ones as well as subplots.

Your story's subplots might align with your main story or present a contrast. For instance, my "Procrastinator" story might include a subplot about travel: "I usually wait until the last minute…except when it's something I *really* want to do, such as planning a vacation—I love to travel so much, I'm usually all packed and ready to go a month ahead of time!"

In addition to depth, subplots can provide clues about what your rewritten story might look like. For instance, if you're generally confident *except* when public speaking, maybe you don't want that to be part of your ideal story—or maybe you do, in which case your rewritten story might be, "I'm growing increasingly confident speaking in public, thanks to Toastmasters and a lot of practice."

We'll explore possibilities for rewritten stories in Part III. For now, let's just consider the subplots that are already in your life and how they might fit in with your big-picture story.

What subplots are part of your story?
What hobbies or other secondary parts of your life aren't directly related to your main story but are still important to you?

How do these subplots relate to your main story?
Do these secondary aspects of your life reinforce the main themes of your life or provide counterexamples to the norm?

Weaving It All Together: Writing the Master Story

Now that you've explored the elements of your story (and your character, your world, and your life) and the common threads that connect them, the time has come to weave them all together into a single, cohesive story—your first draft.

So, take some time to review your story's elements, the common threads, the subplots, and any notes you've taken along the way—and then write a draft of your story, drawing from all the understanding, insight, and clarity you've gained while reading Part I.

You can write the story any way you want, but I'd suggest keeping it relatively short. (After all, the main point is to find, well...*the main point!*) Rather than describing every major episode of your life, look for your big, overarching "master story"—the super-structure rather than the details.

Also, if you're not sure how to start, feel free to use some or all of this template:

> A [character/characteristics or label] in [their world] wants to [desire] because [motivation—general and/or specific], but [obstacles/ challenges/habits]. For a long time [status quo] but then [call to action/ change].

For example, someone using this template might write:

> A single mother in middle-class suburban USA wants to express her artistic talents because she feels an inner yearning (and because she saw her mother frustrated in this area and vowed never to fall into that trap herself), but she fears rejection and doubts her own talent—plus, she's so busy raising her daughter and just trying to make ends meet that she never pursues this calling seriously. For a long time she merely dabbled in art, never showing her work to anyone (and mentally referring to herself as "The Closet Amateur"), but then she got sick, reexamined her priorities, and realized that she didn't want to die with her art still inside her—after all, what sort of role model would that be for her daughter...or for herself?!

(By the way, don't worry if your story doesn't have a happy ending...yet! In Part II, you'll release the disempowering parts of your story, and in Part III you'll give yourself the story you want. For now, this is merely a summary of the way it's been and a snapshot of your soon-to-pass moment—not how it's going to be forever.)

However you decide to tell your story, remember that it doesn't have to be polished or perfect—it's just a first draft. So don't worry about getting it "right"—just get it written!

My Story (First Draft)

Reflect on the dominant elements and common threads you've explored above and weave them together into a single "master story"—a summary of the underlying principle that ties together the elements of your life.

My Story...in a Single Sentence

Summarize the story you told above in a single sentence. (E.g., A frustrated wannabe artist allows self-doubt and fear of rejection to stop her from pursuing her artwork seriously.)

My Story...in a Single Word or Phrase

Now further summarize your story—condensing it into a single word or short phrase (e.g., frustrated wannabe artist).

Congratulations!

You've just completed the first major portion of this book—you've identified your story!

Take a moment to pat yourself on the back for becoming aware of this huge part of your life—for recognizing the most significant elements of your life, tying them together in a concise story, and putting it down in words. This is no small accomplishment—it's a huge step forward on the path of conscious living and personal growth! It also gives you something to work with as you move forward on your journey of transformation.

After you've taken some time to bask in the glow of your completed draft, let's move on to the next stage of the process, where you'll examine your story, get rid of the parts that aren't serving you, keep the gems, and prepare to write a new story that reflects your highest aspirations and your best self.

Part I Summary

Introduction/Overview

Do you ever feel stuck in a rut—thinking the same thoughts, feeling the same emotions, going through the same experiences, and repeating the same patterns (even if the details change)…day after day, year after year? The problem isn't you or your life; the problem is that you've gotten stuck in an old story that no longer serves you…and maybe never did.

The good news is that you can rewrite this story, using the same tools master novelists and screenwriters use to make their stories exactly the way they want—except instead of applying these tools to fictional stories, you'll apply them to your real life.

It might sound far-fetched, but this approach actually works—and I should know because I've used it in my own life and with coaching clients…and I've seen amazing, life-changing results in areas such as health, work, finances, relationships, creativity, and more. And it also can help you break out of your rut, reach your goals, and live the life you want. Beyond that, it will empower you to know that you are no longer at the mercy of other people's stories—or your own. You are the master—and author—of your own life!

Of course, there are many other ways to improve your life—and you've probably already tried some of them. But if you haven't yet gotten the results you want—if you're not living the life of your dreams and feeling the way you want to feel—it may be time to change the underlying cause of your problems: the story you're telling about your life and yourself. As you've probably seen in your own life, if nothing changes…*nothing changes!* You could very easily look at your life one year from now, ten years from now, or at the end of your life and see that you're in exactly the same place you're in right now—with all the same frustrations and unrealized dreams.

But you don't have to be afraid of whatever your own "Ghost of Christmas Future" vision looks like—you can preempt it by rewriting your story…starting now! After all, you were born for something more—a bigger, better story for you, everyone in your life, and the world! By following this book's simple four-part plan (*identify, release, rewrite,* and *live* your story), you can create a story and a life you love.

Steps of Part I: Identify Your Story

Before you can rewrite your story, you have to know what it is! Part I is where you take the essential first step of this process: identifying your story. Here are some key pieces of that process:

- *Recognize that stories have significant consequences.* They aren't just casual anecdotes. They determine your thoughts, emotions, and experiences in all areas. They control your life. It's often easier to recognize this in other people's stories, which can help you take a clearer look at your own.

- *Know your motivation.* People resist change. To take a step as big as rewriting your story, you've got to have a powerful reason to do so. So, what's *your* motivation?

- *Identify the elements.* Before you can put together the pieces of your story, you've got to know what those pieces are—such as anecdotes you tell repeatedly (out loud or in your mind), recurring patterns or themes in your experiences, and significant parts of your current life (including relationships, health, work, and money).

- *Know yourself.* Just like a novelist needs to know their protagonist inside and out, you need to know as much as possible about the protagonist of your life story: *you!* This includes noteworthy traits and qualities, hopes, fears, challenges, beliefs, and self-image (including labels you apply to yourself). Knowing yourself goes beyond looking closely at a "snapshot" of your current life; it also includes seeing how you've changed over time and how you're still changing—in other words, your "character arc."

- *Know your world.* Because no one is an island, you and your story will naturally be influenced by your environment—including your physical surroundings and the social norms, expectations, and rules of the world you live in.

- *Weave the elements into a first draft.* After you've considered these individual pieces, use them to tell your "master story." And remember, this isn't just any old story about one or two isolated parts of your life—this is the story at the core of *every* part of your life, the story that directs your thoughts, emotions, and experiences. The one that defines you, controls you, and in many ways feels like it *is* you. After you write this story, summarize it in a single sentence, phrase, or word.

Looking Forward

By reading Part I, reflecting on the questions, and coming up with your own answers, you've discovered (or clarified) a first draft of your story. But, as with well-written novels, your first draft will not be your final draft. You'll have plenty of opportunity to revise, refine, and rewrite your story until you get it just the way you want it.

Your first draft most likely contains some elements that you like—personal qualities, themes, and other life-story elements that you'd like to keep. And by all means, please do so! The point of the RYS process isn't to ditch it all and start over from scratch in every area of your life. Even if that were possible, it probably wouldn't be desirable!

But if you've been honest with yourself, your first draft will inevitably contain certain elements that don't match your ideal life. Maybe you've uncovered a tendency to sabotage your success, attract unhealthy relationships, live by unnecessary rules that get in the way of your happiness, or some other suboptimal aspect of your life-story. These are the parts that you'd like to release, which is just what you'll do in Part II.

In the pages that follow, you'll revisit your first draft, separate the gems from the junk, and clear the way for a story you actually want to live. How do you do this? Turn the page and find out!

PART II

Release Your Story

*Don't spend your life believing a story about yourself that you didn't write
that's been fed to you—that you've simply accepted, embedded and added to.
Let the story go and there beneath is the real you…and your unique gifts,
heart and path that await you.*
— *Rasheed Ogunlaru*

CHAPTER FIVE

Outgrown Stories

The real challenge for the individual is to practice evolution,
to learn the lessons of the old stories so we no longer need to repeat them.
— Bruce Lipton

AN OLD EPISODE OF *THE SIMPSONS* depicts students signing up for gym class on a first-come, first-served basis. Noticing that Bart and his friend Millhouse aren't around, one of their classmates says, "If they don't get here soon, it'll be T.S. for them!" Answering the obvious question—*what exactly is T.S. (and why is it such a dreaded fate)?*—the scene shifts to a sign reading "Tethered Swimming," below which the hapless Ralph Wiggum struggles to swim while attached by a rope to a poolside pole.

Taken literally, tethered swimming might seem absurd; in a sense, though, it's something we all do: we struggle to move forward yet make little or no progress because we're attached to something—in many cases, an old story.

If you ever find yourself "at the end of your tether"—striving to reach your goals but held back by limiting beliefs or outdated stories—it might be time to cut the cord. In other words, release disempowering worldviews, perspectives on your past that no longer serve you, and, perhaps most important of all, negative labels you still identify with.

Life on Nars?

My friend John once told me about his college buddy who went by the name "Nars." No, this wasn't his birth name, but it's what everyone called him and how he introduced himself when meeting new people. He didn't choose this moniker because it was the name of someone he admired or a fictional hero. It wasn't an old family name or a cool-sounding variation of the Scandinavian name Lars. It was an acronym for "Not A Rocket Scientist."

(Take *that* one in for a moment!)

I'm not sure why he started calling himself Nars. Maybe he wanted to distinguish himself from his bright siblings. Maybe someone said it to him in a mean-spirited way, and he decided to diffuse the situation by turning it into a joke. Or maybe he was the first one to say it, and when he got a laugh, he decided to say it again…and again and again. But, regardless of how it got started, the name stuck. And eventually it became not only a nickname but his identity and his story.

Yes, it's a very short story, but it's a powerful one with far-reaching consequences. Just imagine the many ways in which this label could affect his life, including his self-esteem, the people he hangs out with, and certainly his choice of profession. With a nickname/self-image/story like that, it's safe to say he probably won't work for NASA, nor is he likely to become a Harvard professor, a brain surgeon, or any other job that requires a high degree of intelligence. As a young adult, he'd already boxed himself in—or boxed himself *out*—based on four little letters.

But there's an upside to Nars's story: He illustrates our power to choose our own identity and write our own story. True, he chose a disempowering label/story, but he just as easily could have chosen an empowering one—one that celebrated his strengths and pointed to his potential.

After all, he did go to a fairly competitive college, so he had to have *something* going on upstairs. But even if he wasn't already a rocket scientist, he could have been a rocket scientist *eventually* (although "Arse" wouldn't have made for a very good acronym/nickname—especially among his British friends). And even if he didn't turn his label/story into a nickname, he could have told himself a story about his ability to learn new things, expand into new areas, and become more than he is right now. He could have told himself a story about what a good sense of humor he has. He could have told himself a million different stories that were more empowering than "Nars," but first he had to make room for them...by releasing his old story.

And that's just what you're going to do in this part of the book—let go of any stories that have been boxing you in, holding you back, and keeping you from embodying your highest potential and your best self.

Releasing your old story (or, more likely, just the parts that aren't serving you) will leave you light, free, and ready to create a better life-story for yourself. And it doesn't involve any complicated psychological procedures or esoteric exorcisms; it's a very simple process—one that writers go through every day, every time they hit the Delete key or (for those who still write/edit by hand) pick up the red pen.

When you look at your own story—the one you wrote at the end of Part I—it may not seem as disempowering as "not a rocket scientist." Or maybe it seems worse—like the woman who told me she's unlovable. More likely, it's a mix of positive and negative, or maybe it's an old story that used to be positive but is feeling increasingly negative—a story you've outgrown, like an old pair of shoes. When you look at your story this way, it's not about judging or condemning it so much as finding what fits you now and what it's time to let go of. After all, ask yourself:

Are You Still Wearing Your Baby Shoes?

Do you still walk around in the first pair of shoes you ever had? Probably not, right? What about the clothes you wore when you were a little kid? Are you still trying to squeeze into your first pair of jeans? How about that outfit you thought looked so cool when you were ten years old? Or the one you *didn't* think was cool but had to wear anyway because it was a gift from a well-meaning relative?

I'm guessing that these shoes and clothes have long since been retired from your wardrobe. Not that there was necessarily anything wrong with them. (Although, in retrospect, some of them may have merited an intervention from the fashion police.) But at the time, they probably seemed reasonable enough. Or at least they fit.

But they don't fit anymore. So you stopped wearing them. You handed them down to younger siblings, gave them to Goodwill, or simply threw them away.

It seems obvious enough with physical clothes, but it can get trickier when it comes to inner "clothing" such as beliefs, habits, roles, labels, and stories. For instance, as a youngster, perhaps you played the role of the obedient (or even subservient) child. Or maybe you picked up a belief such as "You can't trust anyone." You might have believed people who said you weren't very bright (or beautiful or talented, etc.).

In some cases, the people who passed down these stories may have been acting maliciously (such as someone telling a child that they're not beautiful). Most of the time, however, these inner hand-me-downs were probably well intentioned. And in most cases, they probably served a valuable function: They may have helped preserve the peace in a turbulent home environment. They stopped you from taking candy from strangers (except on Halloween!). And in one way or another, they kept you safe. But you probably reached a point where these beliefs, roles, and habits no longer served you—yet you didn't replace them.

Let's think again about your first pair of baby shoes. They were probably given to you by your parents. And they probably fit very well (at first). They probably kept your feet safe and protected—especially if you wore them when you first learned to walk. And they were probably adorable! But if you kept wearing those shoes as your feet grew, eventually they wouldn't have been good for you. They would have been painful. They would have given you blisters. Eventually, they would have hindered your development or even crippled you.

Just like these shoes, many of your beliefs were passed down to you by parents or other (usually) well-intentioned adults. Just like these shoes, they kept you safe and served a valuable purpose. Also like these shoes, you've probably outgrown them. The trick is to know when to let them go and update your inner wardrobe.

This doesn't mean that everything you learned as a child needs to be discarded. You probably learned many valuable lessons that will serve you well throughout your entire life. However, you probably also learned some that, like old clothes, fit at the time but no longer fit. (And you probably picked up plenty of inner "clothes" that never fit to begin with!) It's your job as a conscious adult to tell the difference—to distinguish what's a valuable family heirloom that you want to keep, what was once valuable but no longer fits, and what was *always* junk. And then make sure you take the all-important next step:

to replace anything you've outgrown with something that fits the person you are today.

So, when you revisit your story (here in Part II or on your own, beyond this book), look for the parts that no longer fit—the parts you're ready to say goodbye to. This might mean letting go of most of your story, just a few small parts, or perhaps even *all* of it. No matter how much of your story you release, you might find letting go harder than you'd expect. You may feel a tinge of sadness at saying goodbye to a familiar piece of "inner clothing" that may have as much sentimental value as your baby shoes. Or you might feel afraid of giving up your inner security and embarking on a journey of redefinition—or even rebirth. You might even be angry at yourself for staying stuck in a limiting belief/story for so long.

But remember that those beliefs, roles, and other habits probably once served you very well. It's just that you're ready to move on to something that's a better fit for the person you are now and the person you're becoming. Just the fact that you're willing to explore this process is a healthy sign. It means you're ready for an inner-growth spurt!

Throughout the rest of Part II, we'll revisit your story and treat it kind of like spring cleaning for your inner wardrobe, separating the "items of clothing" (i.e., parts of your story) you want to keep from those you're ready to let go of. Before you dive into the specifics of your story, though, take a moment to reflect on your life and ask yourself...

What inner "baby shoes" have you been wearing?
In other words, have you maintained any long-standing beliefs, roles, habits, or thought patterns that no longer serve you? How have they impeded your personal growth? What new "inner clothes" would be a better fit for the person you are now...and the person you're becoming?

What outdated labels have you been identifying with?
Do you use any descriptions or nicknames for yourself (even in your mind) that don't fit the person you are or the person you'd like to become? Are these labels that used to fit you but no longer do, or (like "Nars") did they never serve your best interest? What labels might serve you better?

What's your tether?
Have you ever felt that, despite your efforts, you struggle to move toward your goals? If so, what inner "tether" might be holding you back? (For instance, do you have low self-esteem, core beliefs that conflict with your aspirations, or a story that doesn't lead to your desired destination?) How can you cut this cord and free yourself to move forward?

Feline Case Study: Monkey Wastes Eight Years on a Story

I've already shared several examples of stories that deserve to be given the old heave-ho—such as "I'm not a rocket scientist" and "I'm unlovable because I'm flawed." You can probably think of a story from your own life that you'd like to release—a story that's been harming you or holding you back from the life you want.

As you reflect on your story (or the parts of it that aren't serving you), please don't get down on yourself for having this story in the first place. You're certainly not alone in repeating a story that keeps you from living your fullest life. As Gay Hendricks writes (in the passage quoted at the beginning of Part I), "Almost all of us have a story about why we don't access our genius." In fact, I can tell you from personal experience that humans aren't the only ones who tell ourselves self-detrimental stories. Our cat, Monkey, told himself a story that robbed him of joy and friendship for eight years—a time that should have been the best years of his life.

Monkey and his four littermates were born in a snowstorm but, fortunately, were rescued by a nice man who took them in, kept them warm, and, once they were old enough, made sure that they and their mother all ended up in loving homes. We adopted Monkey and his brother Biddle when they were ten weeks old.

For the first two years of his life, Monkey was playful (with us and with Biddle), friendly (even with our dog, Xena), and snuggly—he was a real mama's boy who loved to climb under the blanket for naps. But that all changed when Elsie arrived.

We found Elsie in a vacant lot near our house, and when no one responded to our local and online "Found Cat" notices, she became a permanent member of our family.

With all due respect to our wonderful boys, we couldn't have asked for a better cat than Elsie. Right from the start, she was friendly, loving, gentle, completely nonaggressive, playful without being rowdy, and about as low maintenance as a cat could be (content to spend most of her time just sitting quietly near us). Like Monkey, she was a tabby; but when we found her, she was only about half Monkey's size (although her love of canned food eventually brought her within a few pounds of him…and earned her the nickname "Hogletina"). If ever Monkey wanted a friend, Elsie seemed made to order. However, he didn't see it that way.

In Monkey's mind, Elsie was the enemy. He attacked her every chance he got, even though she never instigated anything and never fought back. (Her biggest "self-defense" move was to squint and flinch away from him, which meant that it was up to us to break up their daily one-sided fights.) More perplexingly, Monkey's entire personality seemed to change. He stopped participating in our nightly play sessions (sulking by the back door while Biddle and Elsie romped with their toys) and no longer showed up for nap times. Occasionally, we'd get glimpses of the old "Baby Monkey"—snuggling with him on the couch or on a cat blanket—but only when no one else was around. As soon as Elsie walked into the room, he would tense up, stop snuggling, and, more often than not, attack her.

Although some readers might accuse me of anthropomorphism, it seemed quite clear that Monkey was telling himself the story that Elsie was his enemy, and he couldn't let down his guard around her, show any sign of vulnerability, or let her "catch" him being a mama's boy. And, like so many of the stories we tell ourselves, it was completely fictitious—yet he made it true by believing it.

Sadly, after eight years with us, Elsie suffered a stroke and passed away suddenly. And just as suddenly, Monkey's personality reverted to the way it had been for the first two years of his life. Immediately, he started snuggling with us again—joining us on the couch, resting his head on Jodi's leg, and even climbing onto her lap for the first time since he was two. He also played more in the next eight days than he had in the previous eight years! For us, we had lost a beloved daughter and friend; but to Monkey, the danger had passed, and he could finally let down his guard and just be himself again.

Jodi and I were grief-stricken from the loss of Elsie, and we were also saddened by the loss of so many good years for Monkey. He'd spent the prime of his life—from ages two to ten—depriving himself of joy, would-be friendship, and the ability to relax and just be himself. And it all could have been completely different if he'd just told a different story.

To make Monkey's story even more poignant, exactly seven months after Elsie died, Monkey also passed away suddenly and unexpectedly, from an aggressive form of cancer. This loss compounded our heartbreak and also drove home the price of telling yourself a story that keeps you from your best life.

A Growth Mindset and Opposable Thumbs

I'm sorry for this double-downer, but I hope that some good comes from sharing this cautionary tale. Perhaps it can serve as a reminder that you don't have to wait for a death to change your story. You can decide *right now* that you're ready to stop wearing your baby shoes, stop defining yourself with labels that don't represent your highest self, and stop repeating stories (out loud to others or silently to yourself) that don't support the life you want to live and the person you want to be. You can do this because you have two things that (with all due respect to our beloved furry son) Monkey didn't have: a growth mindset and opposable thumbs.

As psychology professor/researcher Carol Dweck describes in her book *Mindset*, we can train ourselves to have more of a "growth mindset" (believing we're capable of improvement) as opposed to a "fixed mindset" (believing we're trapped by our innate abilities and limitations). Without denying our current reality, we can change our story to a more empowering one simply by adding the words "not yet." With this approach, "I'm not where I want to be" becomes "I'm not *yet* where I want to be." "I'm not a published author" becomes "I'm not *yet* a published author." And "I'm not a rocket scientist" becomes "I'm not *yet* a rocket scientist"!

So, as you revisit your story, please don't get discouraged because it's not the story you want to tell and live. That doesn't mean it's a permanent fixture in your life. It just means it's not *yet* the story you want—the story you *will* tell and live at some point in the (hopefully) not-too-distant future!

And remember that, in addition to a growth mindset, you also have the advantage of opposable thumbs! Unlike my cat, you can literally pick up a pen, cross out parts of your story that you don't want to keep, and write new words that you *do* want to make part of your story and your life.

And that's exactly what you're going to do in the next chapter as you review your story, pick out which parts you want to keep as is, which parts could use a little revision, and which parts you're ready to release altogether.

CHAPTER SIX

Red-Pen Power

The story of your past doesn't have to become the story of your life.
— Luminita D. Saviuc

AS A CHILD, CATHY RECEIVED MIXED MESSAGES about financial success. On the one hand, it was a worthwhile—albeit difficult—goal. On the other hand, rich people were jerks! These confusing, contradictory stories were reinforced regarding other areas of success as well. For instance, she was encouraged to do well in school but never praised for doing so: her parents didn't acknowledge her straight A's with even so much as a "good job."

In early adulthood, she kept trying to impress people in order to get attention, which led to some success but not a feeling of fulfillment. As a young "go-getter," she quickly advanced in her career as a project manager, but her big dreams always seemed to elude her.

Now in her fifties, Cathy is more comfortable setting her own definition of success, which includes publishing her creative writing, working from home, and feeling comfortable with herself rather than seeking external validation. Also, after seeing many wealthy people generously giving back to their communities, she has a much more positive view of them—and of wealth/success in general—and embraces prosperity in her own life. (She's even developed a love of golf, which she'd previously been told was a stupid game for rich jerks!)

Even as she's consciously rejected old stories, however, she acknowledges her continued ambivalence about them. "Although I brought my kids up to believe they can accomplish anything they want, I wasn't brought up that way," she says. "Even though I know it, I'm not sure I *feel* it." Nonetheless, she has moved far beyond her childhood stories and, because of her, the next generation is poised to continue this progress.

To translate Cathy's journey into RYS parlance, we could say that she's edited her story—for herself and for her children. She's kept some parts (such as "success is worthwhile") while releasing what doesn't serve her or her children (such as "success is difficult" and "rich people are jerks").

It's taken Cathy most of her life to make this revision (which is still in progress), but you don't have to wait years, decades, or an entire generation to replace old, disempowering stories with new ones that help you become your best self and live your best life. You can start making changes in your story—and your life—immediately. To take the first step, you just have to pick up one of the most powerful tools for writing, editing, and living:

The Red Pen

Remember our analogy of the red pen and the blue pen? The blue pen is great for creating (brainstorming, taking notes, and writing a first draft), and the red pen is great for editing (correcting mistakes, deleting weak spots, and strengthening parts you want to keep). But it's impossible to write with them both at the same time, and if they're constantly fighting over who gets to write, nothing will get done at all!

That's why I encourage you to start with the blue pen only, and if the red pen tries to muscle its way in (e.g., through your inner critic telling you all the things you're doing wrong and how you should improve your story), tell it—politely but firmly—that now isn't its time. It will have its turn to take control when the time is right, but not during the creation process.

This is a key distinction for writers and editors—and *especially* for writers who edit their own work. After all, if a creative writer allowed their inner editor to stick in its two cents after every word they wrote, they'd never finish anything (as many frustrated writers know all too well!). You can drive yourself nuts trying to edit your story while (or even before) you write it. You can stymie your creative process through premature judgment. You can stifle yourself through self-doubt or "analysis paralysis." And you can suck the life (and the fun) right out of your story.

But this doesn't mean the editor isn't valuable—it is! Editing is an essential part of the creative process. Without sorting through your words, making sense of them, analyzing and, yes, even *judging* them, your words might remain no more than a jumble of random thoughts, impressions, and free associations (like unexcavated gold mines). Which doesn't mean that they're not valuable—just that you need to sort through them ("mining for gold") in order to discover their true value.

And that's where the editor comes in—right now.

After all the writing, creating, and self-discovery you did while identifying your story in Part I, it's now time to put down the blue pen, pick up the red one, and find out how to turn the story you've story *got* into the story you *want*. In other words, it's time to edit.

I know, I know—many people feel their stomach drop as soon as they hear the word *edit*. It takes them right back to the bad old days of grammar school, facing a stern-faced, red-pen-wielding pedagogue ready to pounce on every linguistic peccadillo with the force of a ruler rapped against the knuckles. This approach to editing can drain the blood from your face, your knuckles, and your writing!

(Plus, many of the so-called "rules" enforced by these militant grammarians [a type famously lampooned by linguist Theodore Bernstein in *Miss Thistlebottom's Hobgoblins*] are nothing more than outdated, nonsensical, or baseless prejudices, idiosyncrasies, or common superstitions—the linguistic equivalents of urban legends. But that's another topic altogether.)

Rest assured, however, that this is *not* the type of editing we're talking about here. We're talking about constructive editing—the kind that actually improves your writing. The kind that builds on the beauty already in your story and removes anything that detracts from it. The kind that results in a fuller, more radiant expression of *you*.

I won't lie, though; editing isn't always easy. You may have to sift through a lot of dirt, junk, and rubble. But in the process, you'll probably discover some previously unmined gold—material you can pull out, polish, and carve into a priceless treasure! And throughout this process, you (not me, not Miss Thistlebottom, and not the person who instilled the story in you) always have the power. You get to decide what to keep as is, what needs a bit (or a lot) of polishing, and what you want to throw away forever—which is often the most liberating and empowering part of the whole RYS journey.

So, no matter what you may have thought about editing in the past, you'll soon see that when you apply it lovingly to your own life story, it's one of the best ways to get you from where you are now to where you want to be. And it all starts with taking another look at your story, which we'll do right now.

First Pass, First Impressions

Like writing, editing is a multi-step process. Editors go through many "passes"—reading a story for different reasons, looking at different levels of detail. During the first pass, editors don't generally worry about small things like spelling or grammar; instead, they just take it all in and feel their initial reaction to the story in general.

You can do that right now as you begin to review your own life story. Before you start analyzing or getting bogged down in tiny details, it's useful to take a quick look at the first draft and record your initial impressions.

Take some time right now to review what you've already written and—without over-analyzing—see how you feel about your story's first draft.

What are your first impressions?
Reread your story's first draft, which you wrote in Part I, and write down your thoughts, feelings, or general impressions about it.

Second Pass: Sifting and Sorting

After reviewing the story once, focusing on the big picture and general impressions, look at it again with a discerning eye for detail. Specifically, see which parts you definitely want to keep, which parts you definitely want to delete, and which parts you're on the fence about—or might like to make some changes to without getting rid of altogether.

For instance, let's say this is your story:

I'm an achiever. I accomplish wonderful things that I'm very proud of. However, my drive for achievement gets in the way of developing close, meaningful personal connections. My workaholism has stood in the way of would-be romantic relationships and has even created rifts and distance with friends. In several cases, my overzealous drive (and long hours and the physical/emotional distance connected to my work) has hurt people I care about deeply, which hurts ME.

You'd probably like to keep the first two sentences: *I'm an achiever. I accomplish wonderful things that I'm very proud of.* And you'd probably want to completely delete several parts of the story, such as "workaholism," "rifts and distance with friends," and hurting others and yourself.

Also, there may be parts with potential—parts that you may be able to rework into a desirable form. For instance, "drive" can be a very positive quality…if applied with a healthy balance (without the "overzealous" qualifier).

Now it's your turn to start the editing process. Grab your red pen, take a look back at your first draft, and make your mark (or *many* marks, most likely).

Keep, Change, or Delete?

As you reread your story's first draft, indicate (with a red pen—or any other color) the parts you'd like to keep, change, or delete. Also feel free to make notes in the margin (or in the space below)—such as ideas for future drafts.

So, how did the editing go for you? Was it helpful to look at your story with slightly more distance? Were you able to see it more clearly, perhaps even with a degree of objectivity?

Even if you're not usually a huge fan of editing, you might find that it can be a very rich and rewarding process. Not only does it (hopefully) improve your writing, but it also allows time for self-reflection—a time to clarify your message, your style, and your values (what's important to you and what isn't).

And when it comes to editing your real-life story, there's another huge benefit: It shows you that your story *can* be changed, that it isn't written in stone, and that you have the power to mold it any way you want! This may come as a revelation to you if you've always felt that your story is "just the way it is" (or "just the way *I* am") and there's nothing you can do about it. By stepping back and examining your story with a degree of distance and objectivity, you see that you're not trapped in it. You cease to be a helpless character stuck in someone else's drama, and you become the empowered author/editor of your own life.

When you look at a story from this perspective, it's often very clear to see what's working and what isn't. But what if your story isn't as cut and dry as my example of the workaholic? What if you're not sure what to keep, what to change, and what to delete? How do you know which parts of your story have merit, which parts have potential, and which parts are beyond help? How can you use your red pen to bring out the best in your story…and your life?

This is where the all-important third pass comes in—when we really get down to business.

Third Pass: Cost-Benefit Analysis

Yes, it's great to be aware of your first impressions and then take a second look at your story, but let's not stop there. After all, if you're going to be getting rid of some parts of your story and keeping others, you want to know why you're doing it. You want to take a clear-eyed look at how your story is helping you and how it's hurting you, how it's moving you toward your ideal life-story and how it's holding you back.

To put it in business terms, before you decide to keep, delete, or change your story, you want to analyze its costs and benefits. A business performs a cost-benefit analysis (CBA) to determine whether a project is worthwhile, and you can do the same thing with your story.

You might not think of it in these terms, but cost-benefit analysis is nothing new for you. You already do this in every part of your life, every single day—whether you're aware of it or not: you weigh the costs and benefits of your words, actions, and decisions, as well as the stories you tell…and live. You ask yourself (consciously or not): *What am I getting from this story? Is it costing me more than its worth?* Unlike most businesses, however, you look at more than just the financial costs and benefits—you consider your emotions, psychological well-being, and every aspect of your life (an approach that, come to think of it, could serve as a good model for business CBAs as well).

Presumably, you already know that telling (and retelling and reliving) your story costs you *a lot*—otherwise you wouldn't want to change it, and you wouldn't be reading this book! Perhaps your story costs you in terms of health, relationships, success, or self-esteem. Or perhaps it has opportunity costs—positive paths you didn't take because they conflicted with your story. (For instance, perhaps you didn't follow your desire to paint because you told yourself the story, "I'm not very artistic.") In one form or another, you must feel that your story is interfering with you living your best life.

But your story also has to benefit you in some way—otherwise, you never would have started telling it. Some part of you must have realized that there are advantages to telling, retelling, and holding on to your story. And that part isn't likely to relinquish those benefits without a struggle—or at least striking a deal. (More on that later.)

So, before you decide whether or not to release your story—along with its costs and benefits—let's see what exactly you might be giving up and what you'd rather keep.

Stories with Benefits

We've already looked at how every character (and real-life human being) needs a motivation to act, and this is certainly true for you. There must be benefits to taking the actions you take, making the decisions you make, and living the way you live. You need a compelling reason (or reasons) to tell and live your story. So, what are your reasons? What benefits come with your story?

If you're telling a very positive story, the benefits may be obvious. For instance, the story "I'm a money magnet" might have the benefit of making you rich. But what could be the benefit of a negative story—such as "I'm accident prone" or "I get sick a lot"—especially one that has left you with years' worth of wounds or scars? Can *wounds* have benefits?

Yes, they can! In fact, they have both inner and outer benefits. When you have a physical wound, it's often very apparent. For instance, if you break your arm, everyone can see the cast. So the costs and benefits are fairly clear: Yes, it hurts; but you also get attention and sympathy. People want to sign your cast. They ask if they can carry your books. They wish you a speedy recovery. Despite these upsides, however, in this case, you'd most likely say that the costs far outweigh the benefits—given the choice, you probably would *not* want to break your arm!

But when you have an inner wound (or even a physical wound that's no longer visible—or never was) the only way to get any benefit is by telling people about it—telling your story over and over again. You might even get benefits simply by telling the story to yourself.

For instance, a story about a wound unfairly inflicted on you might help you deflect responsibility. A story about how you have a hard time learning new things gives you a free pass to avoid the hard (or possibly not-as-hard-as-you-think) work of learning. The story/label, "I'm not a risk-taker" let's you off the hook for never taking a chance. And retelling any story at all reinforces your existing worldview—it "makes you right." (And who doesn't enjoy being right?!)

Each time you tell your story (to others or to yourself), you receive some benefit—a little "hit" of sympathy, attention, comfort, or some other satisfying reaction. It's almost like a trained animal pressing a lever to receive a pellet of food. Every time you tell your story, a little "pellet" of sympathy (or some other benefit) appears. Even if retelling the story is painful, it must also bring a pleasurable benefit that outweighs the pain—otherwise, you wouldn't tell it!

I know that my story about procrastination has cost me a lot, but it's also provided me with some serious benefits: Waiting until the last minute gets me focused and working more efficiently than I would do for a project that isn't time sensitive. While I'm in pre-deadline panic mode, I give myself a free pass to blow off all non-urgent matters (such as dealing with bills and other such unpleasantness). I also get an adrenaline rush followed by a satisfying sense of relief (or even elation) when I'm able to make a deadline. Also, right up until the last-minute panic sets in, my procrastination story/habit lets me be lazy. It lets me reap the (temporary) benefit of the adage: "Hard work may pay off in the future, but laziness pays dividends *now!*"

To get back to our writing/editing model: even a very problematic first draft probably has some good parts that you'd like to keep in the final version. Maybe you'll leave those parts as is, or maybe you'll rework them into other forms. The first step, however, is to identify the good parts—the benefits of your story as it is right now.

In Part III, we'll figure out how to keep the good parts of your story and receive the same benefits *without* reverting to the negative parts of your story. (As I mentioned earlier, there's a part of you that's going to be very reluctant to relinquish your story's benefits—but that part would probably accept a deal: getting the same benefits, or something better, from a different source.) But before we start figuring out what those alternative sources of benefits might be, let's look at the benefits of your current story. In other words, let's see if you can identify the "pleasure pellets" that your story provides.

What benefits have you received by telling (and living) your story?
For instance, has it let you off the hook, providing a built-in excuse to be irresponsible, unadventurous, or just plain lazy?

What enjoyable reactions has your story elicited from others?
For instance, do you get sympathy or a feeling of bonding with people who share similar stories (no matter how self-limiting these stories may be)?

What enjoyable internal experiences have you had while telling your story (to others or just to yourself)?
For instance, do you feel a sense of pride, a sense of being right, a sense of self-righteous indignation, or a sense of identity?

Meeting Your Needs

There are innumerable benefits you might derive from telling a story—for instance:

- You might get a "free pass" or all-purpose excuse that lets you off the hook from hard work or responsibility.
- You might get to play the "poor me" card and get sympathy.
- You might get attention (positive or negative—it's still attention).
- You might get to avoid rocking the boat with longtime friends or family members who know your story—and might feel confused, skeptical, hurt, or even threatened if you changed.

On a deeper level, beyond specific benefits, there's a good chance that your story fulfills one of more of your core needs.

Ardrey's Core Needs

Addressing this issue in real life as well as in works of fiction, anthropologist and screenwriter/playwright Robert Ardrey identified three core needs that all people (and realistic characters) share: *identity*, *stimulation*, and *security*.

Does your story fulfill any (or all) of these three needs? For instance, here's how my "Procrastinator" story might fill these needs:

- *It provides me with an identity.* I'm "The Procrastinator" (which comes with built-in membership to several other unofficial clubs, such as "Slackers" and "Underachievers"). It also provides an identity by way of contrast with everyone who finishes their tasks comfortably, with plenty of time to spare (the human equivalent of "product differentiation"—extreme procrastination is [or *was*] something that sets me apart from others).
- *It creates stimulation.* Procrastination manufactures drama by forcing me to rush, creating stress and tension and resulting in a sense of relief—*if* I'm fortunate enough to meet my deadline. (I've never jumped out of airplanes, scaled mountains, or even driven significantly above the speed limit—so procrastination has provided about as close to a daredevil adrenaline rush as I get!)

- *It provides security.* As undesirable as this identity/situation may be, at least I can count on it. I've been there before; I know this routine, this game, this *story*. For better or worse, The Procrastinator is "the devil I know."

What about you? How does your story fulfill these core needs?
Identity:

Stimulation:

Security:

Maslow's Hierarchy of Needs

You can also think of your story as fulfilling areas of the "Hierarchy of Needs" developed by famed psychologist Abraham Maslow. Here are the levels of need that he identified (from highest to most basic):

- *Transcendence** – helping others achieve self-actualization
- *Self-Actualization* – personal growth, fulfillment, reaching your potential
- *Aesthetic** – appreciation of beauty, balance, harmony
- *Cognitive** – the desire for knowledge, meaning, and intellectual stimulation
- *Esteem* – confidence, status, achievement, respect
- *Love/Belonging* – family, friends, relationships, and tribe
- *Safety* – security, law and order, stability, protection
- *Physiological* – bodily needs: food, water, sleep, etc.

* These three areas, not included in Maslow's original hierarchy, were added to later models.

Even a story you want to change is probably filling your needs on one or more of these levels. For instance, the story, "I'm a hard-working family man who doesn't have time for art" might fill the lower four areas, whereas a "starving artist" might sacrifice those areas in exchange for self-actualization and aesthetic satisfaction. On the other hand, a self-described "absent-minded professor" might be motivated primarily by cognitive and transcendence needs. They want to help their students blossom while satisfying their own intellectual curiosity through research and learning—but they don't believe that they can do this while also remembering where they left their car keys! And *any* story can provide a sense of belonging by helping you bond with others with a similar story (such as in support groups for alcoholics, cancer survivors, veterans, or many other shared experiences/stories).

All these needs are important, and all of them are perfectly valid motivations for creating, telling, and living your story. Take some time to reflect on how they relate to your own story (including which areas you tend to focus on—or neglect) and see if this model helps you understand your motivations, needs, and desires a little more clearly.

What needs from Maslow's Hierarchy are filled by your story? How?
Transcendence:

Self-Actualization:

Aesthetic:

Cognitive:

Esteem:

Love/Belonging:

Safety:

Physiological:

Play It Cool

I have a slightly different take on the question of benefits and needs. Although it may not sound as profound or psychologically sophisticated, I feel that a major motivation for telling our story—or for anything we say or do— is the desire to feel cool.

I know it probably wouldn't make the most impressive topic for a PhD dissertation; nonetheless, I believe that the desire to appear cool (to others and, perhaps even more importantly, to ourselves) exerts an incredibly strong pull on us—influencing our actions, our attitudes, and our stories.

Even if you no longer think your story is cool, you probably did when you started telling/living it. And before you knew it, you were hooked. (Think of the teenager who starts smoking to look cool—and ends up continuing the habit for decades, perhaps while trying to quit.)

But coolness (or at least *attempted* coolness) and long-standing habits don't just apply to chemical dependency. With my story, for example, at some point I must have picked up the notion that procrastination was cool. Or, more likely, that being organized and planning ahead was uncool. After all, the students who finished their term papers a week early were nerds and dweebs. People who filed their taxes in January were uptight squares. I wasn't one of "those people." I was a rebel—shootin' from the hip. I was cool. (At least in my own mind!) That's why I didn't start my term paper until the night before it was due. (How cool can you *get*?!)

Perhaps that story served my self-image at one point—allowing me to identify with the "cool" slackers rather than the uncool nerds. Now, however, I think it's significantly cooler to finish projects ahead of time rather than stress over every little deadline. I'm still motivated by a desire to be cool—I just have a very different idea of what's cool and what isn't. (Now, it's more along the lines of "calm, cool, and collected.")

Consider your own story and how it's fulfilled your desire to be cool, and then answer the following questions (if that's cool with you):

A Cool Story

How has your story helped you feel cool?

How has your idea of what's cool changed since you first began telling your story?

What about your story still seems cool to you?

What parts now seem uncool?

What Else?

Aside from core needs and general benefits you've identified above, what specific benefits have you received? Or, to put it in fiction-writing terms: what about your story motivated your "character" (you) to act the way they did—and to repeat their story/actions for so long?

With my story, for instance, I've found that procrastination has let me off the hook (in my own mind) where quality is concerned. For instance, when I've waited until the last minute, it's enough of a victory just to complete a project—never mind completing it *well!* I didn't have to concern myself with excellence or reaching my full potential. I could be content with "good enough" (or simply *done*) rather than pushing myself to be great. Also, it forced me to be efficient (a good skill to have—especially if it could be applied in non-emergency situations).

What about you? What benefits has your story provided for you?

Additional Benefits

In what other ways (aside from those mentioned in the sections above) have you benefited from your story?

Summary of Benefits

Now that you've explored your story's benefits from a number of different perspectives, summarize the primary benefits. In other words, what are the main parts of your present story that you would like to keep?

In editing terms, identifying your story's benefits is like highlighting your best passages—the parts you want to keep (either as is or in some revised form). We'll revisit these benefits in Part III, when you'll rewrite a story that still delivers the desirable benefits, meets your core needs, and keeps you cool (by your current standards). For now, however, what's most important is that you've been able to recognize that you *have* benefited from your story and that you've identified some of those specific benefits.

Let's not forget, though, that your story brings more than just benefits—it's costing you...a lot! (Otherwise, as I've already noted, you wouldn't be reading this book.) In fact, I would guess that if you ran a personal cost-benefit analysis on your story, you would find that the costs far outweigh the benefits. So, just as we've explored your story's benefits, let's take a clear-eyed look at its costs.

Counting the Costs

A disempowering story can cost you in many areas of your life. As I've pointed out, my procrastination story hurt my emotions, finances, health, relationships, and self-esteem. And that's just what I was aware of! Who knows how many opportunities I missed because of procrastination? Who knows how many doors were closed to me because my rushed work wasn't as good as calmly produced work would have been? (Or countless other scenarios: opportunities missed while I was in a production panic, people who didn't want to hang out with me because I seemed stressed, or potential business partners who were turned off by my bad work habits.)

I'll never fully know how much good stuff I missed out on, but I do know that my story came with costs that far outweighed the benefits.

Let's take a look at what your story has cost you in the past, what it's costing you right now, and what it will continue to cost you if you don't rewrite it.

Known Costs

What has your story cost you throughout your life (in terms of hurt, loss, or pain)?

Opportunity Costs

Even if you can't know for certain, what opportunities might you have missed because of your story?

Present Costs

What is your story costing you right now?

Future Costs

If you don't rewrite your story (and release the harmful parts of it), what might your story cost you in the future—in terms of pain, as well as missed opportunities?

Summary of Costs

Just as you did for benefits, summarize your story's primary costs. In other words, what aspects of your story would you like to release?

Cost-Benefit Analysis

How do these costs outweigh the benefits of maintaining your story?

Diagnosis ≠ Cure

Now you can see just how much your story costs you, why those costs outweigh the benefits, and why you should release the parts of your story that don't serve your best interests. You've got it all written down in black and white (and red all over—if you've been editing!).

But just seeing this is not enough to change your life. (As I frequently say: *Diagnosis is not cure.*) That would be like saying you can heal a broken arm just by realizing that it's broken—or that realizing that a relationship is toxic fixes (or ends) the relationship. Clearly, it doesn't—although it is a critical first step. But now it's time to move beyond diagnosis. The time has come to break up with the negative aspects of your old story and say goodbye once and for all.

CHAPTER SEVEN

Saying Goodbye and Letting Go

What you're telling is just a story. It isn't happening anymore. When you realize the story you're telling is just words, when you can just crumble up and throw your past in the trashcan, then we'll figure out who you're going to be.
— Chuck Palahniuk

HAVE YOU EVER BEEN in a toxic relationship? One where you knew you weren't good for each other, where you brought out the worst in each other, and where you wanted out but for some reason you stayed?

How about a so-so relationship? Or a vaguely dissatisfying one? Or one that was decent but not great—that didn't bring out the worst in you but also didn't bring out the best in you, serve your higher needs, or fulfill your deepest desires?

How about a relationship where you wanted your partner and/or the relationship itself to change significantly? And, if nothing significant changed, did you stay in the relationship anyway—long after the point when you knew it was over (or, rather, long after it *should* have been over)?

If so, *why?*

(If not, consider yourself fortunate! And keep reading anyway—since, for now, we're just looking at relationships as an example of the patterns and stories we get stuck in.)

Why wouldn't you just break up with a partner who you knew wasn't a good fit for you? Why would you try to keep a relationship alive long after it had run its course, after it was clear that it wasn't serving one (or either) of you?

There are as many reasons as there are relationships, but here are some possible explanations:

- *Benefits* – No matter how deeply flawed a relationship may be, it must contain some benefits: friendship, companionship, financial stability, sex, or any other desirable element that's mixed into a relationship that has become undesirable overall.

- *Identity* – You might not know who you would be without this relationship. You've been part of this "we" for so long that you've lost your "I." Your life and your identity might be so wrapped up in your "better half" (or even a *worse* half) that you fear that losing the relationship means losing your*self* (as you know it).

- *Comfort* – Even the most deeply flawed relationship is still the known, which offers the allure of comfort. And the longer you stay in the relationship, the more comforting this known element becomes.

- *Fear* – Conversely, it can be scary to dive into the unknown—worrying that you might never again find love (or passion or romance or even companionship).

- *Laziness* – As mundane as it might sound, many people stay in unfulfilling relationships for the sake of convenience. And let's face it— it's a pain in the butt to split up your stuff, find a new place, move out, and start a new life—not to mention custody battles and childcare arrangements if you have kids together! It's easier to stay the course than to head in a brand-new (and unknown) direction.

There are many other reasons why you might stay in a flawed relationship that's run its course. Maybe it boosts your self-esteem to be with a seemingly desirable partner. Maybe you feed off of a volatile relationship's drama and the attention it brings you (especially if it's a frequent topic of conversation with your friends and family—without the relationship drama, what would you talk about?). Or perhaps you've been in the relationship for so long that you've ceased to consider breaking up as an option—it might feel like a fixture over which you have no more say than you do over the weather. (But, of course, you always do have a say in your relationships, just like you always have a say in your story!)

And there are just as many reasons why people stay stuck in unfulfilling stories.

Breaking Up with Your Story

Just as many people prolong toxic relationships or repeat the same relationship patterns with different people, many of us repeat the same old stories in all areas of life. We get stuck in a rut. We develop bad habits. We live out the same storylines in a thousand different ways, even when we know they don't serve us.

So, just like those unnecessarily prolonged toxic relationships, why doesn't everyone just break up with their toxic stories? Probably for many of the same reasons why they don't break up with toxic partners: convenience, fear, laziness, or any of the other factors that keep people stuck in unhealthy relationships, ruts, or stories of all kinds.

And yes, just like it can be hard to break up with a partner, it can also be difficult to "dump" an unhealthy story. However, here are a few factors that make it easier to say goodbye to a story that isn't serving you:

- *You're the sole author* – Unlike a relationship, which is created by two people, a story only has one author—so you get to write (and edit/rewrite) it exactly the way you want it to be.

- *No guilt about breaking someone's heart* – You don't have to worry that you've ruined someone's life, crushed their dreams, or broken their spirit. Your old story isn't going to cry all night if you leave it for a healthier story.

- *You get a line-item veto* – As much as you might love to change certain aspects of a flawed partner, you can't necessarily pick and choose which elements you get to keep and which you eliminate (e.g., saying, "He's such a good father, provider, and lover—I just wish he didn't cheat on me!"). But in a story, you get to do exactly that—which is what we've been doing during this editing process: separating the unhealthy aspects of your story from the beneficial parts. So even if you have a 90% unhealthy story, you can keep the 10% that serves you.

During the next set of exercises, you're going to break up with your story—but not necessarily *all* of it. After all, as we saw in the "Benefits" section, your story isn't without redeeming qualities. Chances are, it's a "fixer-upper"—namely, a deeply flawed story that does have potential but that, in its current form, isn't worthy of you.

So, to use two clichés in one sentence (as a writer, I apologize in advance), before you throw out the baby with the bathwater, separate the wheat from the chaff. Although my former writing teachers would be cringing right now, I hope this gets my point across: pull out the parts of your story you want to keep, and then "break up" with the rest.

Keepers

What worthy aspects of your story would you like to keep? (Draw from your "Summary of Benefits" exercise and add any other desirable qualities that you'd like to stick around—even post-breakup.)

Send 'Em Packing!

What parts of your story would you like to kick out of your life once and for all? (Draw from your "Summary of Costs" exercise and add any other undesirable qualities that you'd like to ditch.)

Dear John

Write a breakup letter to the undesirable parts of your story—explaining why you're breaking up and making it very clear that you *never* want to get back together. As the saying goes, "Don't leave a door where you want a wall." If you never want to see this story again, don't bother with the euphemisms (e.g., "Maybe we should cool it for a while, just take a little break and see how things go"). If you want to say, "Hit the road, Jack," then that's exactly what you should say! You can be kind (e.g., thank it for all the benefits and lessons it's given you over the years) or you can be harsh (e.g., telling it how much havoc it's caused and how you can't stand one more minute together), but don't worry about breaking it gently or hurting its feelings. Just be honest and say what's in your best interest—writing exactly what you want, need, and intend in order to create your best story and live your best life.

So, was that cathartic? Were you able to get a load off your chest? Did you express exactly why you want to end it with your old story—once and for all?

I hope you feel better (and lighter). And I hope you were serious about wanting those negative parts of your story out of your life, because now we're going to take things to the next level of finality…

I'm Telling You for the Last Time

In 1998, Jerry Seinfeld recorded a stand-up comedy special called *I'm Telling You for the Last Time*. In the show, he performed many of his favorite comedic bits that he'd already done over the years—vowing that this would be the last time he'd use this material. When the special aired on HBO, Seinfeld's live performance was preceded by a mock funeral in which he buried his old jokes in a casket, mourned by many fellow comedians.

Now, you're going to perform your own version of *I'm Telling You for the Last Time*—complete with a funeral in which you'll retire your old material and bury the past.

Like Seinfeld, your old stories have probably served you very well. Unlike Seinfeld, you probably never told your story in a sit-com, a Broadway show, or an HBO special, but you probably have told it in many situations to many different people (including to yourself within your own mind). And you've probably gotten a lot of mileage out of that story. Maybe, like Seinfeld, you got laughter. Maybe you got sympathy. Maybe you got an all-purpose excuse. Or maybe you just got the comfort of a familiar story—and the familiar identity that went along with it.

But, as you've seen in the previous exercises, you've also gotten a lot of pain, heartbreak, missed opportunities, and suffering. And you're no longer willing to keep living this way—to keep telling the same old disempowering story. And to demonstrate this unequivocally, you're going to hold a funeral for your story—and lay it to rest once and for all.

Beyond Words

As you know, writing is a huge part of my life. I've dedicated decades to it. I love books. I love stories. I love words.

But I also acknowledge that there's something beyond words: action. When you perform a physical action—even a small, symbolic gesture—it takes the message out of your head. It reinforces the lesson. It brings your words to life.

Part IV will focus mainly on this aspect of your (rewritten) story—applying it to your real, everyday life. But you're going to take an important action right now—something that will extend this lesson beyond the page, reinforce its impact, and apply the power of ritual to the process of releasing your story.

Here's how it works:

- *Write* – First, on a separate piece of paper, rewrite the negative parts of your old story (drawing from the "Summary of Costs" and "Send 'em Packing" exercises, adding anything new you think of).
- *Read* – Next, read your "Dear John" letter out loud.
- *Release* – Then, hold a ceremony in which you bury your written story. Literally, physically bury it—or do something comparable, such as burning it, ripping it up and throwing it away, or flushing it down the toilet.

Feel free to add any additional ritual elements, such as burning sage, playing music (possibly something along the lines of, "Na-na-na-na, na-na-na-na, hey-hey-hey, goodbye"), or anything else that's meaningful and symbolic for you. What you're doing here is sending a very clear message to your old story: *You're gone!*

Completely gone. Out of my life—forever! No going back. No "asterisk" (e.g., I'll never tell this story again*…[*except when I'm at a party and I want to get a laugh, or when I meet someone new, or with close friends, or when I'm drunk]). It's not "sort of, kind of" gone. It's gone. Period.

End of story.

Story Funeral

Perform a funeral for your story—either following the previous suggestions or taking any other ritual action that's particularly meaningful for you...and that unequivocally drives home the point that you're telling this story for the last time, after which it will be out of your life forever. If you'd like, you can take some time beforehand to brainstorm ideas for rituals or actions that might help make this point in ways that you can feel on a deep level.

Reflections on Your Story Funeral

After you've finished your story funeral, write down your reflections on it—such as descriptions of what you did, how it made you feel, and how you're feeling now that the funeral is over and the story is gone.

Time to Grieve

After you've held your story funeral and reflected on it, take time to grieve (just as you'd probably do after any funeral you attended).

This might sound funny—after all, you're letting go of a story that you didn't want—but it's an important part of the process. It's just like you might grieve for an ended relationship, even if you were the one who ended it because it was toxic. Or you might grieve for someone who died, even if you didn't particularly like them, if they had been a big part of your life.

Likewise, even though you've consciously chosen to release the unhealthy parts of your story, it might take some time to process the feelings this brings up. You might go through the classic stages of grief (denial, anger, bargaining, depression, and acceptance), or you might experience something completely different. You might feel confused or empty, wondering, "Who am I without this story?" Or you might not feel much of anything—maybe after burying your old story, you'll feel fine and never look back.

Give yourself time and space for anything that surfaces to come up. And be kind to yourself—experiencing your thoughts and emotions without judgment. No matter how much that old story may have hurt you or how ready you are to say goodbye, it was still a significant part of your life, so it may take some time to reorient yourself in the post-story world.

In the words of Anatole France, "All changes, even the most longed for, have their melancholy, for what we leave behind us is a part of ourselves; we must die to one life before we can enter into another." In Part III, you'll enter another part of your life as you write a new and improved story. But for now, rather than rushing straight into a new story, give yourself time to fully release the old one. Say goodbye (and perhaps good riddance) and allow yourself to feel whatever you feel.

Part II Summary

Out with the Old...

Before you can rewrite your story, you have to make room for it by releasing the old story that's been running your life...so that it doesn't end up *ruining* your life! But you probably don't want to get rid of your *entire* story—just the bad parts. So the first step is to "separate the wheat from the chaff"—namely, identify the parts of your story that benefit you and those that don't. Then, release the negative parts of your old story—ending your relationship with them just like you would (or *should*) end any other toxic relationship. And to make sure that those negative aspects don't come creeping back into your life, perform a funeral—laying the toxic old story to rest once and for all.

Looking Ahead

As the saying goes, "nature abhors a vacuum." So, once you've released your old story, other stories will try to rush in and fill the void. Unlike earlier in your life, however, you don't have to adopt a story by default—passively internalizing whatever story is thrust upon you by your parents, by other significant (or insignificant) people in your life, by your own habitual thoughts and subconscious associations and interpretations, or by the world at large. You can consciously choose to create the story you want—one that serves your best interests and reflects your highest self.

For now, take as much time as you need to grieve your old story, and then move on to Part III, where you'll fulfill the promise at the core of this book: you'll rewrite your story.

Rewrite Your Story

It is natural that by knowing what you do not want, you are able to clarify what you do want; and there is nothing wrong with identifying a problem before beginning to look for a solution. But many people, over time, become problem oriented rather than solution oriented, and in their examination and explanation of the problem, they continue the perpetuation of the problem....
So tell the story you want to live, and you will eventually live it.
— Abraham-Hicks

CHAPTER EIGHT

The Power of Positive Stories

I used to think I was a victim of my story until I realized the truth: that I am the creator of my story. I choose what type of person I will be and what type of impact I will leave on others.
— *Steve Maraboli*

WE'VE SEEN HOW MUCH NEGATIVE STORIES CAN COST YOU in terms of health, happiness, success, and fulfillment in all areas of life. That's why we wanted to eliminate any story (of even part of a story) that falls into that category.

However, stories can also benefit you, support your goals, and transform your life in wonderful ways. You may have already experienced this with some of your own positive stories (or just positive pieces of stories), in which case you can build on these successes. Or, if you've felt hampered by your stories, you now get to create a completely new story—one that fulfills your deepest needs and desires and leads you to your highest aspirations.

If you're skeptical that a positive story can really lead to success and satisfaction, perhaps you need to set your sights a bit higher—or at least as high as the Sistine Chapel's ceiling, where you'll find what may be the most stunning evidence I've ever seen of a positive story's power.

Michelangelo: A Noble Story

As the painter of the Sistine Chapel, the sculptor of *David*, and the architect of St. Peter's Basilica, Michelangelo created some of the greatest artistic masterpieces the world has ever known. He was also the most financially successful artist of the Renaissance. At a time when being an artist was considered a lowly profession, he amassed a fortune worth roughly $50 million by today's standards.

In the book *Real Artists Don't Starve*, Jeff Goins presents Michelangelo as a counterexample to the prevalent myth of the "starving artist." What I find most interesting about this case, however, is the explanation that Goins (along with several art historians) puts forth for Michelangelo's success. Yes, he had talent, ambition, and top-tier mentors—but so did many other artists of his time. What Michelangelo had that the others didn't, however, was a powerful story: "All his life, Michelangelo was told he had been born into a noble family," Goins writes. "This belief guided his understanding of himself, fueling his ambition to become a successful artist.... He was the disenfranchised aristocrat eager to restore his family name to honor." And he certainly achieved these ambitions—creating artistic masterworks, associating with popes and nobility, and bringing honor to his family and himself.

But, as Goins explains, the story has a twist:

> This belief in his own nobility guided Michelangelo, shaping his life and paving the route to his success. But here's the interesting part: it wasn't true. He was not actually from noble lineage, a fact that historians discovered years later. What made him succeed was not a genetic predisposition or some cosmic giftedness. It was how he thought of himself.

If ever there was an illustration of the power of story, this is it! Michelangelo's belief in his nobility may have been a placebo, but—just like Dumbo's "magic" feather (and most real-life placebos)—it worked! As is so often the case, the story became a self-fulfilling prophecy. As Goins concludes, "What we believe about ourselves has a way of coming true—the good *and* the bad." So make sure the story you write, believe, and tell is a prophecy you actually want to fulfill.

But what if you're not as fortunate as Michelangelo, and you don't have an empowering story handed to you early in life (and reinforced throughout your life)? What if your early-life story is terrible—something you definitely *don't* want to live? Are you doomed to live out the self-fulfilling prophecy of whatever story you inherited (or picked up or created), even if it's a negative one? Not at all! At any point in your life, you have the power to take any story—no matter how negative or deeply ingrained it may be—and trade it for an empowering story that fulfills you. This is exactly what my friend Mauri did.

Mauri: The Secret to Happiness

When Mauri was a child, her father left her mother, her sister, and her in a hotel room and never came back. As traumatic as this would be for anyone, it was made far worse because Mauri was told that *she* was the reason this had happened—because she was unlovable and undeserving of love, and no one would ever love her.

Not surprisingly, she took this message to heart. As a youngster, she suffered from low self-esteem, depression, hoarding, self-sabotage, and self-isolation. She saw herself as a constant disappointment and believed that she was worthless, would never amount to anything, would never experience happiness, and would always fail—so there was no point in even trying. In short, she was living out the story told to her as a child.

Then she watched *The Secret*. This movie opened her eyes to the possibility of changing her beliefs through gratitude, vision boards, affirmations, and consistent focus on what she *does* want in her life. She chose to be happy, friendly, and successful. She chose to create a life she loves and to appreciate it.

And she has done just that: In addition to serving as a registered nurse for many years, she now finds deep meaning and satisfaction as an animal lover, adventurer, photographer, speaker, teacher, author, and activist for natural healthcare reform. She lives in a beautiful area near the beach, makes meaningful connections on a regular basis, and loves her life. She's living the happy ending she didn't think was possible before she chose to rewrite her story.

Your Turn

You may not paint like Michelangelo or share Mauri's deep connection with *The Secret*, but you can do something they both did: let a positive story guide you into a life of happiness and success. But unlike Michelangelo (and most people), you're consciously creating that story and making sure it's one you want to live.

You've already taken the first two steps of this process by identifying your old story and releasing the parts that weren't serving you. This clears the way for you to write a new story—one that builds on past successes, benefits from past missteps (or "detours"), and embodies the life you want to live and the person you want to be. Not to be too melodramatic, but I predict that writing your new story is going to be a monumental turning point in your life—perhaps even in the history of the world!

Well, maybe that is a *tad* melodramatic, but I'm completely serious about this being a significant turning point in your life—as long as you decide that it will be...*and really believe it!* Because this is when you get a fresh start. This is when you get to wipe the slate clean and start writing the story of your life—not the way it's always been or the way others think it should be but the way you want it to be. This is when you get to become the empowered author of your own life and rewrite your story.

And you get to have a ton of fun while doing it.

So, let's get started—where every author in history has started every story ever written...

A Blank Page

Some people find a blank page intimidating. And yes, that is one way to look at it. But it's not the only way. Here are some other ways to describe a blank page:

- No limits
- Pure potential
- Infinite possibility
- The starting point of your masterpiece
- Unconditional authority
- *Carte blanche* (literally, French for "blank paper")

Or you can imagine a blank page as being like one of these situations:

- Imagine that, after years of drowning in debt, you wake up one morning completely debt free. Your credit cards are all paid off, as are your car payments, mortgage, student loans, or any other expenses/debts you may have accrued over the years. And your credit is now perfect. Your past is behind you. You have a clean slate. A fresh start. *A blank page!*

- Imagine that, after years of being confined to your bed with physical pain and illness, you wake up in perfect health. You feel great. For the first time in years, you can get up, move around comfortably, and do whatever you want. *A blank page!*

- Imagine that you wake up one morning, look out at your driveway, and see a gift from me to you: a brand-new car! I've left it with a full tank of gas, an Atlas/travel guide and GPS system, a back seat full of food and supplies, and a credit card with no limit (which I'll cover 100%). Furthermore, I've made arrangements to take care of all your work and other responsibilities for as long as you want. So you can go anywhere and do anything you'd like—anything at all. *A blank page!*

This part of the book is your blank page.

This is my gift to you. And although you might prefer the car, trust me when I say that this blank page is infinitely more valuable (if you choose to make it so, that is) because on this blank page, you can write whatever you want. (And then, as you do the exercises in Part IV—if not sooner—you get to live it.) You can put a new car on your blank page. Or better health. Or improved finances. Or new attitudes. New relationships. New beliefs. New confidence. New *anything!*

Your past is behind you. Your future is full of endless possibilities and limitless potential. You are fully empowered to create the life you want to create, to go where you want to go, to write the story you want to write, and live the life you want to live. You truly have *carte blanche.*

No limits. No caveats. No catch.

Not so bad, eh?

So, where do you want to go? What do you want to do? What story do you want to write?

I've got all sorts of suggestions and writing prompts to stimulate your creativity and help you explore your numerous (actually, *infinite*) possibilities. And we'll get to many of them in the coming pages. But before I ask any leading questions or try to steer you in any particular direction (the writing equivalent of "Wouldn't you like to drive west? I've heard the coast is nice this time of year."), I'll let you see what comes to you on your own. I'll let you start to fill your blank page the way that *you* want to.

So, quickly now (before your inner editor has a chance to start second-guessing your creative-genius writer), grab a pen and write down any and all possibilities for your new story. Don't worry about whether or not it's realistic or likely or practical or *anything*. Just explore the possibilities—and remember that this is *your* story, so *anything* is possible!

Blank-Page Freewrite/Brainstorm

Write down any and all positive possibilities for your new story—ideas, attitudes, externals, internals...anything at all. Write quickly, without stopping to think, censor, second-guess, or talk yourself out of anything. Make it a lightning storm of creativity and possibility! Don't worry about spelling, grammar, or even making sense. Just move your pen and let the dreams flow out.

A Better-Than-Blank Page

So, how did that feel? Did you enjoy opening your heart to the limitless possibilities, letting your imagination run wild, and recording your thoughts as fast as you could move your pen? Was it exhilarating? Intimidating? Somewhere in between? A bit of both?

I know I made some pretty grandiose analogies (comparing a blank page to a new car, perfect health, unlimited funds, and unlimited potential), but the truth is, your situation isn't exactly like starting with a blank page.

It's *better* than a blank page!

It's better because you have all the benefits of a blank page (you can create anything), but you're not starting from square one. You're starting off with the huge benefit of having learned from your previous stories and experiences!

Remember all those benefits you identified in Part II (the parts of your old story that you didn't bury, burn, or flush down the toilet)? Well, you get to draw from them as you write your new story. But you're not beholden to them (or anything else from your past)—they're merely options that are available to you.

You also have the benefit of knowing what you'd like to avoid—what pitfalls you've already stumbled into, pulled yourself out of, and know how to steer clear of in the future.

In short, you have the dual benefits of hindsight and foresight.

Plus, you've already been through the story-writing process, so you're not a beginner. The biggest difference, however, is that in Parts I and II, you wrote a story based on your past. Your imagination didn't have free rein. You were tied to the facts. It was more like being a reporter than a novelist. Now, however, you're no longer tied to the past. You get to make up the story that you want! You get to imagine, dream, and create.

From What Is to What If...

In this section, you'll shift from describing *what is* to pondering *what if...*

- What if I didn't have to work?
- What if I got paid (a lot) to do what felt like playing?
- What if I were more confident?

- What if I could be totally myself…and people loved that person—loved the true me?
- What if I could do what I love *and* be wildly successful?
- What if my relationships became deeper and more satisfying?
- What if I could accomplish my biggest goals?
- What if I just felt better…without needing a reason?

…or any other possibility that might appeal to you. It doesn't mean you'll pursue every one of these possibilities (or that every one you do pursue will manifest completely)—it just means you're open to them. It means you don't shoot down these possibilities just because you don't already believe them.

After all, reading, writing, and enjoying good fiction often involves a temporary suspension of disbelief. And the same is true for writing the story of your life. So, as you write, don't worry about whether or not something is true, false, or even *possible*—just open yourself to considering: *what if it were possible?*

Prescription for a Great Story

To put it another way: what you've written so far has been descriptive. (That is, it's been a description of the way your story and your life have been.) What you're going to write now will be *pre*scriptive. In other words, you get to *prescribe* the way you want your life to go. You get to create a story (or "script") that you'd like to write, read, and live.

You might associate the word *prescribe* with doctors—prescribing medicine and other treatments. And this does make a good analogy: you get to prescribe for yourself whatever you feel is most beneficial for your best/healthiest life-story. But the word wasn't always associated with medicine. It actually originated with writing—literally meaning before (*pre-*) something was written (by a *scribe*).

Your old story was already written. (In Parts I and II, you basically just *transcribed* an existing story.) But the new story has yet to be written, so you get to *prescribe* it. As author of your own life, you get to determine the direction of your story. You get to choose what to include, what not to include, what to focus on, and how to tell the story. You get to write and live by declaration. And you get to start right now.

CHAPTER NINE

Writing Your New Story

Do you wait for things to happen, or do you make them happen yourself?
I believe in writing your own story.
— Charlotte Eriksson

NOW YOU'VE REACHED THE HEART OF THE JOURNEY. This is where you get to experience the best of all worlds—creating a new life story that draws on your past successes and strengths while avoiding past missteps. By the end of this chapter, you will have culled the highlights from your past, present, and imagined future and woven them into an empowering new story that you like to tell and *love* to live!

As exciting and enjoyable as this process may sound, it might also seem a bit daunting. After all, this is your one big chance to steer your life in the direction you want to go in, so you'd better not blow it, right? Wrong! This is most definitely *not* your "one big chance"—because you'll have as many chances as you want or need. This is merely the first draft of your new story. And just like a novelist can revise their manuscript as much as they want before publishing it, you'll have plenty of chances to edit your own story—throughout Part III and throughout your life.

This is your time to take the pressure off, explore the possibilities, enjoy the creative process, and savor the experience of being the empowered author of your life.

Elements of Your New Story

Now that we've taken the grand view of your situation (creator of your own life-story, explorer of limitless possibilities, imbued with limitless power, *carte blanche*, etc.), let's get down to details. We'll start the same way we did when we identified your old story: by exploring the elements.

You probably remember the elements we discussed in Part I: themes, messages, catch phrases, etc. Now we're going to revisit these elements but with one major difference: You're not going to describe your story (the way it is or the way it's been); you're going to *prescribe* the way you'd like it to be. In other words, you're going to create it.

In the exercises that follow, you'll revisit the story features we've already discussed, but this time you'll write down the elements the way you might like them to appear in your new story-in-the-making. For example, when you're listing characteristics of your "protagonist" (you), write down the ones you'd like to embody (even if you don't...yet)—such as:

Confident, Disciplined, Optimistic, Creative, Enthusiastic, Generous, Authentic, Joyful

...or any other qualities you'd like to consciously bring into your life-story (or magnify, if they're qualities you already possess but would like even more of).

When you're writing down possible themes, regardless of what themes you focused on in the past, think about which ones you'd *like* to focus on from this point on. For instance, you might write down:

Inspiration, Community, Heart-based Interactions, Strength, Loving Relationships

...or any other theme you think might make for an inspiring story—the kind you'd enjoy writing and, more importantly, living.

Your responses aren't supposed to be accurate representations of your life-story as it's been or even as it is now. These are aspirational responses—musings about appealing possibilities for the life-story you're creating.

And remember, you're not locking yourself into any of these elements—just exploring the possibilities. Later, you'll return to these elements, pick and choose which ones you like the most, and use them as building blocks for your new story. But for now, you're just brainstorming. So let your imagination soar...and enjoy the ride!

Your Dream Character

We'll start with your "protagonist." What are your highest hopes, dreams, and aspirations for the person at the heart of your story (you)?

Let's revisit some of the same topics and questions from earlier in this book, but instead of answering based on the way you've been, answer in terms of your hopes, wishes, and most appealing possibilities for the new you—as if they were already the "now you"!

Qualities

What are some of your protagonist's most positive character traits (e.g., kind, creative, charming, confident, intelligent, funny)?

Labels, Part 1: A Positive Appositive[1]

What labels accurately—and *positively*—fit your character? These could be defining characteristics (e.g., a real go-getter), roles and activities (e.g., a generous philanthropist) or accomplishments (e.g., a bestselling author).

---

[1] An appositive phrase provides information that describes or identifies the word next to it. These phrases can be negative (e.g., "a misguided student" in "Nars, a misguided student, has an unfortunate nickname") or neutral (e.g., "my sister's roommate" in "Lisa, my sister's roommate, is moving out soon"). For your aspirational story, however, you're going to give your protagonist some of the most desirable, positive appositives you can imagine.

Labels, Part 2: Homeric Epithets[2]

How would an epic poet describe the heroic protagonist of your life? Write down self-descriptive words/phrases that accurately (and heroically) reflect your highest self. Then, circle the one you're most excited about. In other words, if you had to choose just one epithet for yourself, what would it be? (Remember that this is the description of your ideal character and life-story— the way you'd like to live, even if it doesn't describe you 100%...yet!)

Self-Image

How does your character view him- or herself? What do they think about their appearance, age, intelligence, abilities, accomplishments, or other major aspects of their lives—or about themselves in general?

Skills/Talents

What is your character particularly good at?

Highest Hope(s)

What does your character wish for most deeply in their heart of hearts?

---

[2] Epithets are labels, nicknames, or short descriptions that convey someone's essence or, at least, a noteworthy aspect of their character. Although they've been used widely for thousands of years, they're often associated with the epic poet Homer (author of *The Iliad* and *The Odyssey*). He used many recurring epithets to describe gods/goddesses (e.g., "wide-seeing Zeus"), mortals ("swift-footed Achilles"), and nature ("rosy-fingered dawn"). Some characters are described by multiple epithets, such as Odysseus, who is alternately referred to as "much-enduring," "man of action," and "great teller of tales," among other descriptive phrases. Now, as the author of your own epic story, you get to create your own heroic/Homeric epithets!

Attitude

How would you summarize your character's general attitude toward life (e.g., relaxed, optimistic, confident)?

Catch Phrase

If your character had a catch phrase, what would it be? This can be any phrase/sentence that you'd want the "character" you're now creating to say or even just think fairly often (e.g., "I'm so blessed").

Worldview/Philosophy

How might your character complete the sentence, "The world is..." (e.g., good; loving; divine; a place for growth, connection, and fun)?

Values

What's most important to your character?

Beliefs

What does your character believe about life, religion, and people (including themselves)?

Character Arc

What are some ways in which your character might like to change, grow, and evolve in the future?

Story Elements

Now that you've thought about who you want your lead character to be, consider some possible elements for the new story-in-the-making that this protagonist will be the star of. Write down whatever you might want in your life in the future...and right now!

Recurring Themes
Write down the themes of the story you'd like to create/live.

Message
Gandhi said, "My life is my message." If you were to say the same of the life-story you're creating right now, what would you want that message to be?

Your World
How would you describe the world you'd like to inhabit (your environment/milieu and the people you'd like to associate with)?

Rules
What rules govern this world (the if-thens, dos and don'ts, and other assumptions)? (For example, "The love I give comes back to me tenfold" or "If I share my heart vulnerably, people respond with love.")

Other Elements?
What other elements might you like to include in your ideal story? Are there any particular scenes you'd like to live out? Goals you'd like to accomplish? Qualities you'd like to embody? Qualities you'd like in a partner, friends, or other people in your life? Anything else?

Better Benefits and Satisfied Needs

By this point, you've already identified many pieces you may (or may not) use in your new story. When the time comes to put them all together, you're going to have a wonderful assortment of characteristics, elements, and other details to pick and choose from and piece together any way you'd like.

In addition to the ideas you've already come up with through brainstorming/writing various story elements, you've also got a big, important area of story material that you've already written: your previous story's *benefits*.

Remember in Part II when you edited your story and separated the costs from the benefits? Well, that wasn't just an exercise in proofreading—that was a way to highlight benefits you might like to include in your new story. Chances are, though, you'd like to revise *how* you receive those benefits.

For instance…

- If you used to get attention through illness, now you might like to get attention because of your talents.

- If you made yourself valuable to others by always going to their agendas and putting their needs ahead of your own (and possibly running yourself ragged in the process), perhaps you could provide value in a balanced way—by nurturing yourself, filling your own cup, and giving from the overflow.

- If you used to get your heart racing by putting yourself into dangerous (or panic-inducing) situations, now you might create excitement by pushing yourself beyond your comfort zone in safe, healthy ways (e.g., speaking or singing in public, publishing your writing, or sharing more authentically/vulnerably with loved ones).

…or any other way that you've attempted to boost your self-esteem with limited (or no) success.

And remember that self-esteem truly is the ultimate benefit we're all striving for. Whether you're writing fictional characters or observing real-life people (including yourself), you'll find that we're all motivated by the desire to increase our sense of self-worth (even if our methods don't always lead to the desired results, as is all too frequently the case). But now you have the chance to revise your methods while maintaining the worthy goal of feeling better about yourself, in whatever specific form that may take for you.

Keep in mind that by doing this, you're not reverting to your old story; you're finding ways to get the same benefits *without* reverting to your old story. You've already thrown out the "bathwater" (the negative parts of your old story), but you get to keep the "baby" (the benefits).

So, what are some ways for you to reap the same desirable rewards without the undesirable elements? Take some time to revisit your benefits (by looking over what you've already written and reflecting on any additional benefits you can think of), and then find new, healthier routes that will lead you to them.

Benefits Worth Keeping

Write down your old story's main benefits that you'd like to include in your new story—even though you'll receive them in different ways.

Top Benefits

From your previous list, choose the top three benefits (the ones that are most important to you and that you'd most like to keep), followed by possible ways you might be able to receive the same benefits from a positive story. Be creative and remember that there are usually many ways to reach any given destination (or benefit). Also, keep in mind that you're not committing to any particular path here—just considering your options.

Benefit #1:

New/Improved Way(s) to Receive Benefit #1...for Positive Reasons:

Benefit #2:

New/Improved Way(s) to Receive Benefit #2...for Positive Reasons:

Benefit #3:

New/Improved Way(s) to Receive Benefit #3...for Positive Reasons:

Fulfilling Your Needs in Healthy Ways

In addition to specific benefits, your old story probably filled certain universal needs, such as the aforementioned core needs identified by Robert Ardrey (identity, stimulation, and security) and the needs in Maslow's Hierarchy (transcendence, self-actualization, aesthetic, cognitive, esteem, love/belonging, safety, and physiological needs).

While it's great to have your needs met, you might have been filling some (or all) of these needs through stories that didn't serve your best interests overall. So, just as you did with benefits, let's revisit some of the needs your old story fulfilled and think of healthier ways for you to fulfill these same needs.

For instance, if someone's old story was, "I push myself until I drop!" chances are, they were putting stimulation (or esteem or other needs) ahead of physiological needs (e.g., getting enough sleep)—until they got sick and were forced to slow down. Perhaps they could meet the need for sufficient rest by taking regular "health days" (to rest and recharge) rather than waiting until their body gave out and forced them to take a sick day.

(Note: Just because it's on the bottom of the hierarchy, please don't neglect or minimize the importance of basic physiological needs, such as proper rest, nutrition, and physical care. These form the foundation for everything else.)

What about you? What appealing stories might fill your core needs?

Top Needs

As you did with benefits in the previous exercise, identify three of your most important needs and think of positive ways to fulfill them.

Need #1:
New and Improved Way(s) to Fulfill Need #1:

Need #2:
New and Improved Way(s) to Fulfill Need #2:

Need #3:

New and Improved Way(s) to Fulfill Need #3:

Something Borrowed, Something You

By now you're getting to be a fairly accomplished writer. In addition to the many notes, preliminary drafts, edits, and revisions you've already written, you've taken some of the most important steps for any writer: mining your past for valuable material and using your creativity to imagine innovative possibilities for your story's future.

But no matter how creative and original a fiction writer may be, they almost certainly draw upon other people's lives for inspiration. And not just people they know—people they read about (real or fictional), people they see on the news, people they encounter briefly, or even people they observe from afar or pass one time on the street and never see again. In short, the entire world and everyone in it is a potential source of inspiration and material. (The phrase "material world" takes on a whole new layer of meaning when used by writers!)

You can take the same approach as you write your own story: As you continue to collect the elements of your story, remember that they don't all have to come directly from you. Feel free to borrow elements from people you know, from people you don't know, and even from the world of fiction. If someone else's story resonates with you, feel free to incorporate parts of it into your own. If a movie hero or heroine inspires you, feel free to co-opt their best qualities for your own "character." If you like some but not *all* parts of someone's life-story, use a "line-item veto": take the pieces you like and ignore the rest. Or, if a person or situation (real or fictional) thoroughly repels you, use the clarity-through-contrast approach: put the exact *opposite* into your story!

Even if inspiration comes from others, the borrowed elements still become uniquely *you* as you work them into your specific story in your own original way.

Can I Borrow Your Life?

Think of people whose lives appeal to you. Then pick the three most appealing ones, summarize their stories, and think about which parts you might like to borrow for your own.

Person #1:

Story #1:

How you'd like to fit parts of this person's story into your own:

Person #2:

Story #2:

How you'd like to fit parts of this person's story into your own:

Person #3:

Story #3:

How you'd like to fit parts of this person's story into your own:

Line-Item Veto: Keep the Best, Toss the Rest

Think of three people whose lives/stories *partially* appeal to you. Summarize their story and identify the parts you might like for your own (discarding or ignoring anything about them that you wouldn't want in your own life-story).

Person #1:

Story #1:

Which parts of this person's story might you like to incorporate into your own life-story? How might this look/feel for you?

Person #2:

Story #2:

Which parts of this person's story might you like to incorporate into your own life-story? How might this look/feel for you?

Person #3:

Story #3:

Which parts of this person's story might you like to incorporate into your own life-story? How might this look/feel for you?

Clarity Through Contrast, Part 1:
Reversing Other People's Unappealing Stories

Now think of three people whose lives/stories are very different from what you'd like for your own life. Identify elements of their stories that are most at odds with your tastes, desires, or values, then think of the opposite of that—a quality that greatly appeals to you and that you might like to incorporate into your own story.

Person #1:

Their Story:

Opposite of Story's Lesson/Take-away:

How you'd like to fit parts of their story's opposites (or the lessons you learned from them) into your story:

Person #2:

Their Story:

Opposite of Story's Lesson/Take-away:

How you'd like to fit parts of their story's opposites (or the lessons you learned from them) into your story:

Person #3:

Their Story:

Opposite of Story's Lesson/Take-away:

How you'd like to fit parts of their story's opposites (or the lessons you learned from them) into your story:

Clarity Through Contrast, Part 2: Revising Your Past

You can also use this process by drawing on your own unappealing experiences. Think of something you went through that you wish had been different, something you regret—a time when something bad happened to you or when you wish you'd said or done something different. With the advantage of hindsight, what do you wish had happened, or what would you have done differently? Or, if you have no regrets and wouldn't change the past even if you could (because *all* your experiences—positive and negative—led you to where you are now and made you who you are), what would you do differently if a similar situation arises in the future?

Experience:

Lesson/Take-away:

Revised Version (of Past Scene or Similar Future Scene):

How could you incorporate what you learned from this into your new story?

Fact and Fiction

The characters and stories that appeal to you (or repel you) don't necessarily have to come from real life; they can come from novels, short stories, movies, or any other type of fiction. Think of an inspiring fictional story and/or character with elements you might like to use in your own real-life story. You can even draw from common themes from fiction, such as "The underdog triumphs," "Good prevails," "True love conquers all," or anything else you might like to be a theme of your story.

Appealing Work of Fiction (e.g., a movie or novel you like):

How you'd like to fit parts of this story into yours:

Appealing Fictional Character:

How you'd like to fit elements of this character into your "character" (you):

Appealing Theme from Fiction:

How you'd like to incorporate this theme into your story:

Unappealing Fictional Story, Theme, or Character:

Opposite of Story's Lesson/Take-away:

How you'd like to fit the opposite of (or lesson from) this fictional story, theme, or character into your story—in a positive way:

Admiration, Envy, Attention, and Curiosity

Another way to figure out what characteristics or elements you might like in your own life-story is by looking at what or whom you admire, envy, or find your attention drawn to. Even a simple feeling of curiosity can be a clue that points toward your ideal story.

For instance, if you have immense respect and admiration for a philanthropist who supports many causes you value, perhaps it's a sign that philanthropy (or related service of some kind) is part of your ideal story. Or if you often find yourself reading stories of spiritual mystics, a similar path might be in your future.

Learning from others doesn't necessarily have to be so noble, however—and that's fine. For instance, if a single person becomes envious at a friend's wedding, maybe it's a sign that a loving relationship (and perhaps a wedding) is an element of their story's happy ending. If you find yourself getting jealous when you hear about someone's new publishing contract (or slim figure, new child, professional success, art exhibit, or anything else you find desirable), there's a good chance that this jealousy is helping you learn more about yourself and your happy ending. After all, if you didn't desire it, you wouldn't envy it!

For instance, if a friend of mine joined a professional hockey team, I wouldn't be jealous—because I have absolutely no desire to become a hockey player. On the other hand, I might feel a tinge of envy if someone I know (or even a fictional character in a book or movie) writes a breakout bestseller, because I would also like that for myself. So, rather than being something negative, I can actually learn from this envy. It brings this desire to the forefront of my consciousness, clarifies the vision of my happy ending, and motivates me to reach it.

One huge caveat in this area, though, is to make sure you're not pushing away what you want by projecting negative feelings toward the people who experience something you want—or by denying your desire out of "sour grapes." Instead, as soon as you become aware of even a touch of envy, you can thank that feeling for alerting you about something you value or desire, thank the person or situation for bringing you this increased awareness, and then create positive feelings and associations with the elements you want to bring into your own life. Good feelings are magnets that lead to more good feelings. So use envy as a wake-up call—and then wake up, write the happy ending you want, and live it!

But even if you're not racked with envy, you can learn a lot about the story you want if you simply notice what you notice. In other words, become more aware of where your attention goes. Whether or not you feel any respect, envy, or anything else, it's definitely noteworthy if you always find yourself drawn to a particular area, person, or situation. Even just being curious about something or someone (thinking about them often, wondering what they're like, etc.) can be a sign that they're part of your own next chapter. So start paying attention to what you pay attention to—and see what you can learn about yourself and the kind of story you'd like to write/live.

When you go to a bookstore or library, which section do you naturally gravitate toward? What types of movies and TV shows catch your attention? What topics come up most often in your conversations? What might these tendencies indicate about your ideal story?

Take some time to contemplate and write about the people you admire or envy as well as the people and situations that most often pique your curiosity or attention, then consider what this might teach you about your ideal story.

Admiration
Who are some people you look up to, admire, or see as role models?

Envy
Have you ever felt jealous of anyone (even just a tiny bit)? Who? Why? What did they do or have that you might like to include in your own story?

Curiosity
Who or what do you often find yourself thinking, wondering, and wanting to know more about?

Attention
Who or what do you find yourself drawn to on a regular basis?

Common Threads, Life Lessons, and Story Elements
What do these objects of admiration, envy, or attention have in common? What can they teach you about yourself? Could any of these lessons, qualities, or elements be worked into your new story?

Reverse Engineering Your Happy Ending

By now you're just about ready to write a first draft of your new story. You've got plenty of raw materials—like a chef with lots of ingredients to choose from, culled from a wide variety of sources. You've drawn inspiration from your own life and also from other people and stories. You know a lot about your protagonist, their arc, and your story's theme.

The final main ingredient to consider is what your story is moving toward—in other words, *What's your happy ending?*

I don't mean the end of your life—just the final scene of this *chapter* of your personal story. It could be a few years from now, a few months from now, or even sooner—whenever you reach your personal idea of success and happiness at this stage in your life. In other words, how would it look and feel if you reached your goal, achieved success, and lived your dream?

Stephen Covey encouraged people to "begin with the end in mind." This is an important reminder when you're working toward any real-life goal, but it's also good advice for authors. For instance, many mystery writers begin by coming up with an ending to their story, then they figure out how to arrive at that end. Romance writers might know that the romantic leads will end up in each other's arms—they just have to figure out what route will get them there. And an adventure writer might know that their hero will succeed in their quest, even if they don't know exactly how.

You can do the same thing while writing your own story. Before you begin writing the first draft of your new story, think of the happy ending you'd like (for the distant or not-so-distant future), then work your way back to the present, figuring out how to arrive at that ending.

In other words, reverse engineer your happy ending.

For instance, if you'd like your story to end with a character winning an Olympic gold medal, think of how they might reach that goal—probably by training almost every day, practicing with a world-class coach, and taking great care of their body. Also, think of the kind of person who would behave this way: disciplined, passionate, dedicated, and driven.

But maybe you don't want to be an Olympic gold medalist. Your happy ending might involve a book contract, a dream wedding, a quietly content family life, or a spiritual awakening and deep sense of inner peace. Whatever your happy ending looks like, begin with this end in mind, then work your way back to the present.

One way to approach this is to imagine that your current life is a movie with a very happy ending. Yes, there may be twists and turns, trials and tribulations, but the final scene shows that you've definitely reached your goals—you're living the life you've dreamed of and worked toward for so long. And the final image—the freeze-frame over which the final credits roll—encapsulates this success.

So, what's the final scene and happy-ending freeze-frame of your movie?

Maybe you're not even sure where you'd like your story to end up. That's okay. You can start with some generalities (e.g., "I feel good") and get more specific as you go along. Or you can mention one or two specifics that you know you'd like (e.g., "I'm happily married" or "My business is a success"), and then fill in other areas of your life later. Feel free to make your happy ending big and bold or something modest if you find that more believable (and less stressful than "shooting for the moon"), remembering that you can always build on small successes during future chapters of your life.

Even if you already have a good sense of what your happy ending looks like, you still may want to embellish, dream bigger (or smaller/simpler, according to your tastes and desires), or simply clarify and fine-tune your vision. In any case, the first step is to get clear about how your happy ending looks and feels—and the following exercises can help you do exactly that.

Elements of Your Happy Ending

What are some internal and external experiences you'd like your story to lead to?

Internals (e.g., emotions, psychological/spiritual states):

Externals (e.g., people in your life, goals you've achieved):

Your Happy Ending

Describe your "scene of success"—in other words, the happy ending you'd like your story to have.

Reverse Engineer Your Happy Ending

Describe the steps that might lead to your happy ending—working your way backward from the ending to the present. (If you'd like, you can do this by imagining talking to your "Future Self"—who's already achieved the success you desire—and asking them, "So, how'd ya do it?")

Your Second First Draft

Now that you've brainstormed, written notes for your new story, and revisited the benefits from your old one, you're ready to write a first draft of your new story.

If this process feels familiar, that's because it is!

And I'm not just talking about the exercise in Part I when you wrote your old story. I'm talking about your entire life. After all, we write our own autobiographies every single day of our lives—by telling stories (either out loud, in writing, or just within our own minds) and then *living* those stories. The only difference between what you usually do and what you're about to do is that now you're going to write your story consciously—deliberately choosing the character, story elements, and happy ending that most appeal to you.

So, take some time to review the elements you've described in the previous exercises, circle the parts you definitely want in your new story, add anything new that comes to mind right now, and then weave it all together to create a story you'd absolutely love to live.

You can do this any way you'd like, but if you want to start with a template, you can use a variation on the one I suggested for your old story:

> A [character/characteristics or label] in [their world] wants to [desire] because [motivation—including the benefits they'll receive]. They're inspired by [people/stories that attract their attention/desire], and they really want to [desired end/goal]. So they [steps from "Reverse Engineering Your Happy Ending"]…and they reach their goal! When they get there, this is what it looks and feels like for them: [inner/outer description of success].

To use a positive variation on our earlier example of the aspiring artist, the new story might look like this:

> A single mother in middle-class suburban USA wants to express her artistic talents because she feels an inner yearning (and because she saw her own mother frustrated in this area and vowed never to fall into that trap herself). She knows that this is her calling because she's felt it for years—and when she put the dream on hold, it kept resurfacing. She knows that if she does express herself artistically, she'll feel great about herself, inspire her daughter, and ideally, support herself and her family as a full-time artist.
>
> She's inspired by Monet and other French Impressionists and by her friend who's a professional sculptor. She'd love to incorporate elements of these artists' work into her own art—but in a modern style that's all

her own. She really wants to take the visions she sees in her mind, bring them to life on the canvas, and make a great living from her art.

She commits herself to making this vision a reality. She takes art classes, paints at least five days a week, goes to museums and gallery exhibits for inspiration, and learns about the business side of the art world. Sure enough, her painting flourishes, the sales start pouring in, she has more time to spend at home with her daughter (who is so proud of her mom!), and she feels great about herself—knowing that she's followed her dream and made it a reality.

Most likely, the specifics of your story will be very different from this. You probably have very different goals. Or maybe you don't even want to focus on specifics but would rather write about a general approach to life (e.g., "I live with an open heart, share freely with others, and radiate joy wherever I go").

Whatever structure or approach you choose, feel free to express big, optimistic dreams and give your story a super-happy ending! This is your blank "canvas"/page for creating the life-story you want. Why not go for the gold?

First Draft of Your New (and Improved) Story

Take the most appealing elements from the previous exercises—including your happy ending, benefits you'd like to receive, characteristics you'd like to embody, or any other elements or ideas you've brainstormed about—and weave them together into a story you'd love to tell...and live!

I hope you've written a wonderful, inspiring, and *fun* first draft of your new story. And I hope it truly is the best of all worlds for you—keeping the best parts of your past and present, omitting anything you don't want, and incorporating elements of the life you aspire to live from now on. This story can also be the best of all worlds in the sense that it's not written in stone; you're not locked into it—so if you revisit it (now, soon, or in the distant future) and find anything that no longer feels quite right for you, you can change it. And if you revisit parts and find that you do still like them, you can keep them exactly as they are or make slight (or major) variations to make them even better! That's the power of the RYS process. That's what it means to be the empowered author of your own story and your own life.

Maybe the first draft of your new story is already just right for you, and you won't change a word. Or maybe, upon reflection, you'll think of a number of changes you'd like to make. Or, even if you're very happy with your story, you might find it valuable to consider alternative elements—just to make sure you're weighing all your options before you settle on the one that appeals to you the most.

In any case, it's always worthwhile to take a step back, look at your work, and consider how (or if) it might be improved. In other words, *edit* your new story—which is exactly what we'll do in the next chapter.

CHAPTER TEN

Editing Your New Story

The secret subject of any story is what we learn, or fail to learn, over time.
— *Robert Penn Warren*

TODAY, PAULA DESCRIBES HERSELF AS "a person committed to self-empowerment," but she grew up believing a story that was anything but empowering: "I am only worthy if I accommodate people." She lived according to this story for many years, but it didn't lead to a sense of self-worth; instead, her negative experiences with being over-accommodating (i.e., a pushover who let people take advantage of her) led her to another detrimental story: "Being nice doesn't pay off."

For most of her early life, these stories prevented her from living as fully, abundantly, and joyfully as she wanted to. Rather than resign herself to a less-than-fulfilling destiny, however, she read books and took courses about self-empowerment, journaled about this topic, and consciously changed her behavior. Ultimately, she emerged with a new story: "It's okay to set healthy boundaries, stick up for yourself, and be self-empowered"—and that's exactly what she now is.

Most people would describe Paula's transition from pushover to self-empowerment as an example of personal growth or self-help. I see it as an example of someone editing their story, which is what you're going to do with your new story right now.

Editing, RYS Style

In the previous exercises, you've let your creative side pour out its highest dreams and visions, unencumbered by the inner editor. Now that you've done that, the editor can step in to help—not to criticize what you've written but to enhance your creativity and move you ever closer to the inspiring story you'd love to tell and live.

As you saw in the Part II exercises, the kind of editing we practice in this book isn't about finding the "mistakes" in your story or pointing out everything you've done "wrong"—it's about giving you a chance to make your story even more appealing to you. It's a way to take the pressure off, to let you know that you don't have to get your story just right the first time. (That's one advantage of story-writing over, say, open-heart surgery, where there actually *is* a lot of pressure to get it right the first time!)

Editing is your friend. It's your teammate, working toward the shared goal of creating the best story possible for you. It's your chance to explore possibilities you may have overlooked the first time around, reinforce parts you already love, and take your story to the next level. And it can actually be a lot of fun!

All kinds of stories get edited—usually several times, for several different reasons. When preparing a manuscript for publication, most editors make multiple passes through a story—checking for different elements with each reading (e.g., starting with big-picture concerns, then making a pass where they check for facts, and finally proofreading for spelling and grammar). In your story, we're not going to worry about spelling and grammar, but we will check to make sure that your story is consistent with your highest values, personal tastes, and other areas of importance.

Let's start with your big-picture impressions and then consider some specifics.

General Impressions

Reread the first draft of your new story (written near the end of the previous chapter) and write down your general impressions of it—including any parts you definitely want to keep, delete, or change in any way. You can also note what comes to mind and how you feel as you read this draft.

First Impressions of Your New Story

What were your general impressions when you read your first draft?

What parts of your draft do you definitely want to keep?

What parts of your draft do you want to delete?

What parts of your draft do you want to change? How?

What other thoughts (general or specific) about this draft come to mind?

Checking for Values

Now let's explore some specific areas of your first draft, starting with values.

Your story might have a wonderful plot that leads to a happy ending, but does it reflect your highest values? For instance, if it's a story of a man who thrives in business and climbs to the top of his profession, but does so by backstabbing and manipulation, that probably doesn't reflect your highest values. That doesn't mean, however, that you need to throw out the entire story and start over. (Again, we can keep the "baby" and throw out the "bathwater.") In this case, you might keep the part about thriving in business, but change the way it's done—perhaps by having the man use his beautiful talents to serve others while loving the entire process.

Take a moment to clarify your highest values, then see if they're reflected by your story.

New Story, Your Values

What qualities or other elements of life are most important to you (e.g., love, connection, family, ease, flow, abundance, creativity)?

How are these values reflected (or not) by your new story?

What changes could make your story reflect your values more than it currently does?

Checking for Appeal

Just as you checked your story to make sure it reflected your values, you can also make sure that the story actually appeals to you. Writing a noble story of a good protagonist who embodies your most cherished values doesn't necessarily mean you'd want to live that *life*. For instance, you might have written about a surgeon who volunteers at a low-income ER, using her expertise to save lives and give back to the community. A great story! A great success! A great example of wonderful values! But you might have absolutely zero desire to be a surgeon.

In other words, it might be a wonderful story…but just not *your* story.

So, take some time to make sure you're writing *your* story—one that reflects your values and also appeals to you and embodies the person you actually want to be.

Character Appeal, Story Appeal

How would you describe the "character" you'd like to be (including their tastes, proclivities, and desires)?

How is this person/character reflected (or not) by your current story?

What changes would make your story reflect your ideal character more than it currently does?

Checking for Story Gaps

Maybe everything in your story is great—it all fits in with your values and really feels like *you*. But that doesn't necessarily mean your story is done. You might have left out a big (or small) chunk of "plot"—leaving a gap that you need to fill in before your story feels complete.

For instance, if the aspiring painter (from our earlier example) wrote her story as, "I decided to be a painter, and then I held my gallery exhibit," she's left a pretty gaping hole in her story: the part about learning to paint and actually doing it!

How about you? Is something missing from your story? Are there any essential links you haven't included yet—or anything at all that would bring your story closer to your ideal? Or are there any "subplots" you might want to add—areas that aren't essential for your primary focus but would nonetheless enrich your life? This is your chance to check.

Also, as you review your story for possible gaps, you can see if it all leads naturally to the ending you desire. If it doesn't, don't worry—simply think of what might bridge the gap to your final "scene of success" or simply add more life to your story.

Mend the Gap
Are there any obvious gaps in your story? How could you fill them?

Subplots
Even if they're not directly related to your main story, would you like to add any "subplots"—elements that make your story and protagonist more three-dimensional? (For instance, would you like to travel, give yourself a hobby, or perhaps a new love interest? Remember, *you* are the author, and this is *your* story—so don't hold back!)

Extrapolation

If you told your new story (in its current form), where would it be likely to lead you in one year, five years, ten years, or beyond?

Happy Ending?

Does this extrapolation lead to the happy ending (or "scene of success") you desire? If not, what changes would make it more likely to lead to the end you want? (Note: Even if it does lead to the happy ending, you can still brainstorm for possible revisions that might allow you to reach this end in a smoother, more enjoyable fashion.)

Proactive Protagonist vs. Deus Ex Machina

One more crucial element to check for while editing your new story is a proactive protagonist (rather than one who's *reactive* or simply passive). This guiding principle of almost all creative writing—including screenplays, novels, and life scripts—makes for a more interesting character, story, and life.

Yes, there are exceptions, such as the laid-back "Dude" from *The Big Lebowski*, Vladimir and Estragon from *Waiting for Godot*, and the title character of Melville's short story "Bartleby the Scrivener" (whose catch phrase, "I'd prefer not to," accurately summarizes his attitude, which is the polar opposite of proactive). In general, however, the ideal protagonist has powerful desires and takes steps to manifest them rather than just sitting around waiting to be saved by a white knight, a winning lottery ticket, or a *deus ex machina* (a creative-writing taboo meaning "a god from the machine"—based on the custom in ancient Greek plays of having a "deity" hoisted into view by a mechanical device in order to deliver a character from a seemingly unsolvable predicament).

While *deus ex machina* may seem like a laughable artifice to modern audiences, it's easy to see its appeal. Wouldn't we all love a *deus ex machina* in our actual lives? If you're drowning in ever-deepening debt, wouldn't you love to win the lottery? If you experience a tragedy, wouldn't you love to wake up and discover that it was all just a bad dream? If you find yourself in grave peril, wouldn't you love to be rescued by a mysterious hero?

Yes, these fantasies are alluring, but they come at a huge price: *personal empowerment* (which is the primary aim of this book). In grammatical terms, passively waiting for a *deus ex machina* is like objectifying yourself—treating yourself like an object rather than the subject of your story. It's like living a story consisting of only passive verbs and passive sentences. It's like being a feather blowing in the wind rather than an eagle flapping its wings and directing its flight. It's like not being the lead actor—the active agent—in your own life-story but rather the one acted upon…or *not* acted upon.

So, what's the antidote to *deus ex machina*? Personal responsibility. This means that *you*—not external factors or other people—are responsible for your thoughts, actions, emotional and spiritual well-being, and your entire life. Personal responsibility takes many forms, such as:

- Maturity
- Power
- Freedom
- Living from declaration
- Self-identification (declaring who you are rather than letting yourself be defined by externals)
- Self-efficacy (having an internal locus of control—believing that you can influence the outcome of events in your life as opposed to being at the mercy of external factors beyond your control)
- Replacing the symptoms of irresponsibility (such as blame, passivity, apathy, and victimhood) with characteristics of responsibility (such as accountability, self-direction, and self-empowerment)

In terms of the RYS process, taking responsibility means being your story's author (having *authority* in your life) rather than being a passive character whose life is completely determined by the whims of other people and external forces.

Personal responsibility doesn't mean you can control every aspect of your life (and certainly not others' lives). It means you accept responsibility for that which you *can* change—and, as stated in the Serenity Prayer, that you have the courage to change those things (and the serenity to accept what you can't change…and the wisdom to know the difference).

By advocating a proactive protagonist, I'm not saying you have to turn into an action hero, a perpetual-motion machine, or a manic extrovert engaged in constant activity (which can actually stand in the way of the quiet reflection that's so important for making wise, thoughtful, soulful choices—and proactively creating your life). And by advocating personal responsibility, I'm not saying that you shouldn't pray for miracles, surrender to a higher power, or actively reach out for support—from friends, strangers, or anyone/anything else that can help you live your best life. Remember, you don't have to go it alone. There's a whole world just waiting to help—why not avail yourself of all the love and support at your disposal? Asking for help is not abdicating your responsibility. In fact, it's often one of the most responsible things you can do.

What I am saying is that you take ownership of your own story and your own destiny, that you consciously decide how you'd like to live…and then live that way—not as a reaction to others but guided by your own inner voice. I'm encouraging you to pick up your own pen and write your own story (figuratively and literally) rather than waiting for someone to write it for you (which, of course, wouldn't be *your* story at all). As the saying goes: "If you don't have a plan for your life, someone else will." To rephrase that in story-writing terms: "If you don't write your own story, someone else will!" (Or perhaps even worse, maybe they won't!)

So, as you edit your new story, make sure that instead of waiting around for a *deus ex machina*, your protagonist proactively directs the course of your life story and confidently guides it in the direction of your dreams.

Proactive Protagonist
As you edit your new story, how can you make your protagonist even more proactive and empowered?

Ex-Machina
Does your story involve a *deus ex machina*—namely, a plot twist that depends on divine intervention or some other external force beyond your control (such as winning the lottery)? If so, how can you change it so that you take more responsibility for creating and living your best story?

From Good to Great

As you've worked your way through these exercises, you've made tremendous progress toward your goal of creating an even-more-inspiring story for your life. You may have written a very good first draft. You may have answered the question of how to fulfill your needs and benefits in positive ways. You may have drawn inspiration from others and incorporated those elements into your story in original ways. You may have created an appealing story that leads naturally to a very happy ending.

But that *still* doesn't necessarily mean you're done.

I know that by this point you might be mentally, emotionally, and perhaps even physically drained (or at least have a slightly cramping hand). Perhaps you're ready to say "good enough" and leave your new story as is. And you're certainly welcome to do this—knowing that you can always return to the story some other time and make any revisions you want. However, if you've got enough stamina to take one more look right now, I urge you to do so. After all, this isn't just a short story for your local paper; it's the story that may determine the rest of your life—and I'd say that's worth taking your time on, giving yourself the chance to consider numerous options rather than settling on the first (or second) thing that comes to mind.

Remember, finding one viable path or "answer" doesn't always mean you should stop exploring or pondering the possibilities. Yes, your first thought— or first draft—might be good. It might even be excellent! But there might be other excellent options that are even more appealing to you—options you might never have considered if you'd stopped looking after your first response.

So, look back over your new story's first draft once again and consider which elements you can enhance, making them go from good to great. See if you can find preferable alternatives to any elements in this draft. Who knows— although this draft is probably already good (or even great), the next one could be an absolute masterpiece! And since you are writing your life story, after all, why not make it a masterpiece?

Enhancements

What elements of your new story's first draft might be improved upon— namely, what could make them more appealing to you?

Alternatives

Find an area of your first draft that works. Then think of another way that it could *also* work. And then another and another and another. The more alternatives you give yourself, the more options you'll have when it comes to your next draft—so you'll be able to choose the best of the best, which is exactly what you and your story deserve. (As Nobel Prize-winning chemist Linus Pauling said, "The best way to get a good idea is to have a lot of ideas.")

Interpretation: What's the Meaning of All This?

By now, it's safe to say you've gathered all the elements of a great, empowering, life-affirming, *you*-affirming story. You've gone through many steps to get to this point, employing many powers of a great author and editor: writing and rewriting your story, examining it from all angles, and enhancing it to make it the best possible representation of the story you want to tell, the person you want to be, and the life you want to live. But you've still got another superpower in your arsenal, which may be the most powerful one of all: *interpretation.*

With interpretation, you not only get to decide what your story is, you get to decide what it *means.* You get to decide whether a challenge breaks you or makes you stronger. You get to decide whether a setback drags you into a pit of despair or teaches you a valuable lesson that leads to a brighter future. You get to decide not only *what* story you tell but *how* you tell it, which is the heart of the storyteller's power.

This power was observed over and over again by Aaron Beck (widely regarded as "the father of cognitive therapy" and one of the most influential psychotherapists of all time). As Angela Duckworth describes in her book *Grit*, Beck focused on his patients' self-talk and observed that "the same objective event…can lead to very different subjective interpretations. And it is those interpretations—rather than the objective events themselves—that can give rise to our feelings and our behavior." In other words, it's the story we tell ourselves *about* an event—rather than the event itself—that matters most.

The power of interpretation is the power of response (your "response-ability"). And this is what shapes your experience of life more than anything else. Because the truth is, you can't always control what happens—what people do or say to you—but you can decide how to respond.

Having negative experiences or hearing negative stories—about yourself, about others, or about the world in general—doesn't doom you to a life of misery. It's possible to transform those negative stories into a positive life—it's just a matter of how you interpret them and how you respond. For instance, a woman named Christine told me that when she was young, she was told that she was stupid and ugly and was never going to amount to anything. But while some people might have turned those messages into self-fulfilling prophecies—giving up on their ability to succeed and, most likely, taking out their resentment on others—Christine said that they led her to be more persistent, compassionate, and nonjudgmental. No, her experiences weren't particularly positive, but through a positive response, she grew to trust others, believe in herself, and feel that she has something valuable to contribute to the world.

As we've already seen in our examples—and as you've probably observed in your own life—writing (or telling) a story of any kind goes far beyond merely laying out the facts. It's about choosing which facts to write about. And which ones to focus on the most (or the least). And your attitude toward them. And how you discuss them. And how you connect them. And your point of view (or "POV"—an abbreviation you'll almost certainly see again and again if you read books on writing, especially screenwriting). And the significance you ascribe to the facts. And, perhaps above all, your interpretation of those facts.

Literary critics, reviewers, and English professors frequently offer differing interpretations of books. This doesn't mean that one of them is right and the others are wrong. It simply means that a story means something different to each one, based on their particular perspective, tastes, experiences, and readings (or, as deconstructionists would say, "misreadings") of the text.

But interpretation begins with the person telling the story—which, in this case, is you! As an author (or storyteller of any kind), you get to do far more than present "just the facts" of your story; you get to determine your story's meaning. And this is a remarkable power—one that, for better or worse, can entirely transform your story and your life.

There's no such thing as a purely objective story. For instance, a supposedly objective newspaper shows its bias simply by publishing a story, which indicates the belief that this story is more important than those they *didn't* publish. Even a history textbook brings a specific POV to the material. (For instance, what American textbooks refer to as the "American Revolution" might be seen as a "Civil War" from the British POV.) Even in casual, everyday conversation, the words people use, their tone of voice, body language, and everything about the way they present their stories clearly convey their attitude toward the material—it conveys what they think the story means. (For instance, depending on how it's said, "Can you believe this cost $10?!" could mean, "What a great deal!" or "What a rip-off!")

The same thing is certainly true about the stories you tell yourself. For instance, if a stranger yelled at you for no apparent reason when you were five years old, you may have developed very different stories around this event, such as:

- I probably deserved it.
- Don't talk to strangers.
- Adults are so mean!
- I've got thick skin—I can handle it.
- They probably had my best interest in mind, even if I didn't realize it at the time.
- They probably had their own issues, which they were simply projecting onto an innocent little kid. It's not my fault, and it had nothing to do with me or my inherent worth as a human being.

(I would guess that if you ascribed the last story, it would have been in retrospect, rather than as a five-year-old...unless you were *extremely* precocious!)

There are many stories you could tell about this or almost any other fact or event, depending on what interpretation and meaning you ascribe to it. And here's the incredibly empowering part of this: although you don't always get to choose the facts, circumstances, and external events in your life, you always get to choose how to interpret them. You get to choose what they mean for you. You get to choose how to *frame* the events.

So, because it's your choice, why not choose the most empowering interpretations possible? Why not tell your story in ways that serve your highest interests, uplift you (and others), and empower you to move forward in healthy ways? Why not choose to put your story in the best possible frame?

And remember, if you don't like the frame your story's currently in, you can always *reframe* it!

Framing and Reframing

In terms of storytelling, *framing* means how you present the material—the context you put it in. So *reframing* means changing the context in which you view an experience. It's seeing the events of your life in a different light, through a different lens, from a different angle—changing your "frame of reference" or your "frame of mind."

Reframing can make the transition from...

- seeing yourself as a victim to seeing yourself as a survivor—or a *thriver*!
- a crisis to an opportunity.
- saying, "I *have* to…" to saying, "I *get* to…"!
- a perceived weakness (e.g., being shy or antisocial) to a strength (e.g., being introspective, sensitive, and self-sufficient).
- a "failed" relationship to a valuable experience that taught you important lessons and prepared you for something (or someone) better in the future.

When applied to your life, reframing is based on a powerful premise: *Your past doesn't define you—YOU define your past!*

Reframing does not mean lying or changing/distorting the facts of your experiences. It simply means seeing them from a different—and (hopefully) more helpful—perspective.

For instance, the would-be painter from earlier examples could tell two very different stories based on her life, depending on how she framed her situation:

> I just turned fifty, and I never did the one thing that I wanted most: pursue art. I just kept putting it off and putting it off, and then one thing after another kept getting in my way, and I never got around to it…and now I never will. It's too late. All the up-and-comers in the art world are in their twenties and thirties. How can I compete with that—or with people my age who have been doing this for decades? Forget it! This whole art thing was never anything more than a pipe dream. I'm worse than a has-been; I'm a never-was! I'm a total failure. I'm a loser. I'm worthless.

Or, here's the same situation put in a very different frame:

> I just turned fifty, and I've never been surer of what I want to do with my life: paint! It's been a longtime dream, and I feel that now is the right time. In addition to my passion for art itself, I'll be able to bring lots of life experience to my work. I've learned so much about life and about myself: what's important to me and what isn't, how to get motivated and focused, and how to get things done. I've also loved, lost, and experienced so much that I know will enrich my work and bring a depth and maturity to it that I never could have expressed when I was younger. This is what I want. I feel the passion, I'm motivated, and I know that the right time is right now. I'm ready to paint!

Sure, both versions of this story could technically be considered "true," but which frame do you think shows her story in the more helpful light? Which frame boosts her self-esteem? Which frame is going to help her get unstuck, reach her goals, and live the life-story she wants?

Obviously, the second version.

Since the painter is the author of her story, she may as well frame it in this helpful light, right? And since *you* are the author of *your* own story, why not frame it in ways that support *you*? Why not interpret the events in your life in uplifting ways? Why not ascribe empowering meaning to your experiences?

As you edit and rewrite your story, keep in mind what it means to you. And remember that you choose the meaning through the way you frame and interpret your story.

Give Yourself an Empowering Frame

What other frames, interpretations, and meanings could you bring to your story? How could you present the same material in a different light? Briefly summarize your story in three different ways from three different (but all positive/empowering) angles.

Frame #1:

Frame #2:

Frame #3:

A Caveat About Reframing

Reframing is one of the most powerful tools you have at your disposal—as a storyteller and in your everyday life. I highly encourage you to put it to use as you rewrite your story, as you bring your best story to life, and for the rest of your life (whenever you sense there's a more empowering perspective to bring to your experiences).

But reframing can also be a double-edged sword (or, to double down on clichés, a slippery slope), so I feel compelled to offer this caveat: Use reframing as a way to tell a *different* story rather than as an excuse to keep repeating the same old story from a slightly different angle.

For example, if your old story was about a "failed" relationship—or a string of "failed" relationships—you could reframe that in a number of empowering ways. For instance, you could consider what you learned from each relationship. Maybe one partner mistreated and disrespected you until you said, "Enough!"—so you learned to respect and stand up for yourself. Maybe the end of a so-so relationship taught you that you don't have to settle. Or maybe noticing patterns repeated again and again taught you that it wasn't just about the other people—that something in you was attracting these partners/situations. And now you can learn from that "something"— becoming more aware, more empowered, and ready to move forward in your life rather than reliving those no-longer-helpful patterns. You're ready to really live!

However, if you keep on telling your "new" story about how you finally said, "Enough!" to a disrespectful partner, you run the risk of making that partner and that relationship a major focus of your current story and your current/future life. This is especially true if you find yourself getting angry when retelling your "new, empowered" story (quotation marks very deliberate). Retelling a story—in *any* frame—might be an indication that you're still holding on to the past…and a particularly undesirable piece of the past, at that! With all the people and things you could choose to focus on, is this *really* where you want to put your attention? Is this really the most empowering topic for you to think about and talk about (regardless of your angle or frame)? Is this how you'd choose to define yourself?

If you've studied or practiced the Law of Attraction, you probably know the danger of the double negative. For instance, if I tell myself an anti-procrastination story (e.g., "Don't procrastinate! I need to stop procrastinating! I'm no longer a procrastinator!"), what key word am I pounding into my subconscious mind? Clearly, *procrastination*. I might kid myself that it's okay because I've reframed the story (and yes, to an extent I have: changing the angle from "I procrastinate" to "Don't procrastinate"), but the key word is the same, the theme is the same, the subject matter is the same, and there's a good chance that the energy is the same. So the *story* is essentially the same; I've just changed a detail.

My story is still about procrastination, which means that *I* am still about procrastination. And, to quote one of my favorite lines by David Foster Wallace, "Defining yourself in opposition to something is still being anaclitic on that thing, isn't it?" (By the way, *anaclitic* means *psychologically dependent*. I had to look it up, too—and, despite my initial confusion, I'd be hard-pressed to think of a more appropriate word for this important point.)

In Part IV, as you adapt your new story from the page into the real world of your daily life, we'll revisit the idea (and practice) of reframing. But for now, as you write one more version of your story, be mindful of the double-edged power of reframing—and use this tool wisely!

Writing Your "Final-for-Now" Draft

So, after all those rounds of preliminary drafts, edits, and interpretations, the time has finally arrived to write a final draft of your new story. Well, not exactly *final*, since as long as you're alive, you can always revise your story, but "final for now"—a version that's worthy of who you are now and your highest aspirations for the future, a version that you're ready to take out and "test drive" in the real world.

By this point, you've considered a wide range of story elements: anecdotes, labels, character traits, character arcs, story world, values, costs, benefits, morals, messages, subtext, subplots, frames, interpretations, and so much more. In fact, you've got so much material that it might even start to feel overwhelming at times. If it does, remember that you don't have to employ every literary device in your ever-expanding bag of tricks, and you don't have to include every detail of your life in your story. If you just focus on what's most important to you and write from your true heart and authentic self, you can't go wrong.

Your Story

Picking and choosing from the elements we've discussed so far in the book—as well as your earlier drafts, edits, and notes—write a new version of your story, one that you'd be thrilled to tell and, more important, to live.

Pitching Your Story

Summarize your proposed life-story in a nutshell, as if you were pitching it to a Hollywood producer—but not just any producer: one who, instead of producing movies, produces real lives. If you had just a few minutes to give them the gist of your story—the main character, the plot, why it matters, and why it's compelling—what would you say?

Producing Your Story

If you were the producer who heard the pitch you just described, would you be interested in this story? Do you find it compelling—a story you'd be excited to read, produce, and *live*? Would you buy the rights to it, or would you pass? What revisions might make it more appealing to you? (Keep in mind, you're not trying to make a blockbuster movie—which would usually have lots of drama, tension, conflict, inner demons, external obstacles, and perhaps a car chase or two. You're trying to create a personally fulfilling life!)

Is Your Story Done...or Just Beginning?

Both! Now that you're done writing (and editing and interpreting and pitching) your new story, you're ready to take it to the next level: beyond the page. In other words, you now get to *live* your story!

John Lennon said, "A dream you dream alone is only a dream. A dream you dream together is reality." To paraphrase this for our situation, we could say that a story that stays on the page is only a story, but one that goes beyond the page is a *life*.

And that's what we'll focus on in the fourth and final part of this book: turning your masterpiece story into a masterpiece life.

Part III Summary

Parts I and II of this book deal primarily with *what is*—the existing parts of your current life and your past. Part III, on the other hand, is aspirational—it's where you turn your attention to the life you want to live and the person you want to be. It's where *what is* becomes *what if*—as you consider the possibilities for the life-story you're creating. It's where you write your new story—not one based on the past, how you've always been, or how other people say you should live, but based on your personally empowered declaration of who you choose to be and the story you choose to write and live.

The main steps in this process are:

- *Embrace the power of the blank page (and the better-than-blank page).* Starting a new story with a blank page (literally and figuratively) means that you get to explore a world of infinite possibilities, limited only by the power of your imagination. However, your situation is even more empowering than this because you get to draw from the past when (and *only* when) it's helpful, draw from other people's (or fictional characters') most appealing stories, and start fresh in any ways you choose.

- *Revisit the elements and revise the benefits.* Return to the story elements you've already explored and reexamine the benefits you received from your old story but do so in a different context: as part of a new story that you consciously choose—one that lifts you up, serves your highest self, and fulfills your deepest desires.

- *Reverse engineer your happy ending.* Envision your scene of success, and then think of how you might be able to reach it. (And remember, there are many possible routes to almost any given point.)

- *Write your second first draft.* Drawing from all the elements and exercises you've explored so far, write a first draft of your new story.

- *Edit your new story.* Review your new story's first draft and think of ways to make it even more compelling, more empowering, and more *you*.

- *Use the superpower of interpretation.* Remember the "superpowers" of interpretation and reframing—telling a story from a new frame of reference, which can drastically change the story's meaning and energy.

However, make sure you don't use this as an excuse to stay stuck or fixated on an old, disempowering story.

- *Write your "final-for-now" draft.* Picking and choosing from all the elements and tools at your disposal, write the story you'd love to tell and live.

Looking Forward

In Part IV, you'll take your story beyond the page, finding ways to incorporate it into your everyday life. This is the step that makes this book more than a mental exercise or a creative-writing manual. This is where you turn your glorious story into a glorious reality. This is where your dreams really do come true.

PART IV

Live Your Story

Make your life a story worth telling. You only get one shot at this existence, and one day when you're gone the most important thing you'll leave behind is the legacy of the life you lived. Make sure you make it a story you're proud to have others tell.

— Adam Braun

CHAPTER ELEVEN

Adaptation: From the Page to the Screen (of Your Life)

You're the narrator, the protagonist, and the sidekick.
You're the storyteller and the story told.
— John Green

HAVE YOU EVER READ THE CHILDREN'S BOOK *Harold and the Purple Crayon* by Crockett Johnson? If not (or if it's been a while and you could use a reminder), it's about a young boy who draws pictures with a purple crayon. But there's a magical twist to this story: Everything he draws becomes real. He draws pies that he can actually eat. He draws a boat that he actually sails on the water. And at the end of this perfect-for-bedtime tale, he draws a bed in which he lies down and goes to sleep.

This may seem like a childish fantasy, but it's based on a real-life principle: The things you imagine and create *can* become real parts of your life! You may not draw pictures with a magical crayon, but you do tell stories with your words—and those stories have an uncanny way of coming true.

Your situation also parallels another one of my childhood favorites: the *Choose Your Own Adventure* series. These are books you don't just read front to back; instead, every time you reach a significant decision point, you choose which option to follow. As much freedom as this provides for the reader, however, your real life provides even greater freedom because: 1. you're not just reading and choosing options but also writing the different possibilities, and 2. you don't just select a path from multiple-choice options but from *unlimited* choices. You can literally write any story you want!

By now, I hope you've written a story that's so wonderful that you would not only choose it but also, like Harold, wish for it to come true. In this final part of the book, we're going to explore ways to do exactly that—to take your story beyond the page and make it part of your everyday life. In the pages to come, I'll share many tools to help you with this process, but first let's take a look at an example of how one person's new story opened the door to a new life.

Bella: From "Not Good Enough" to Reaching Her Dreams

The messages Bella received early in life etched a very bleak story in her heart: "I'm not lovable, I'm not good enough, and I don't deserve good things." Early experiences with neglect and abuse merely reinforced these messages, exacerbating her already low self-esteem. Seeking external validation, she became a people pleaser and conformed to others' expectations of what she should think, what she should do, and who she should be. "I didn't follow my heart or my dreams," she says. "I was sad and depressed on the inside but put on a mask of happiness. I became what others wanted me to be so they would love and accept me. I lost myself."

However, her story and her life began to change when she made a simple yet powerful decision: she decided to learn to love herself. She told herself the new story that "I am good enough and worthy of good things," and before long, her life began to reflect that. After years of believing that it was pointless to even pursue her dreams, she began to *reach* them. Her list of accomplishments in recent years is simply staggering: In addition to earning her Bachelor of Holistic Health Sciences degree, she's become a bestselling author, coach, teacher, and healer certified in numerous modalities. And, as of this writing, she's nearing completion of a Doctor of Medicine program.

Despite her achievements, however, she still feels the tug of old stories, as she often worries about letting others down or being seen as a failure or a fake if she's not perfect and doesn't have all her "stuff" together before she puts something out for the world to see. Nonetheless, unlike earlier in life when her limiting beliefs kept her playing small, she now continues to move forward with her dreams, regardless of doubts. As she says, "It's hard to overcome years of conditioning and reprogramming false belief systems, but it is possible." Her life is a testament to that fact.

Bella's new inner story manifests outwardly in the form of holistic healing, academic achievements, and numerous certifications. Mauri's new story (inspired by *The Secret*, as described in Part III) manifests in the form of travel, public speaking, and activism. Michelangelo's story manifested itself in the form of artistic masterpieces. And your unique story will manifest in its own unique way.

Just as there are infinite stories, there are infinite ways for them to manifest. What's most important is that they actually do manifest—namely, they don't just stay on the page or in your mind; they become part of the real world, which is the ultimate goal of this whole process.

Taking Stories Beyond the Page

Here's a (sort of) weird thing about this book: The title is *Rewrite Your Story*. Each part contains numerous writing and editing exercises. We explore examples from many types of writing—from novels and screenplays to songs and stand-up comics. And we employ numerous literary tools and principles to help you become a better author.

But here's a (not-so-secret) secret: This isn't a book about writing. It's not *Creative Writing 101* or *Introduction to the Novel* or *How to Write a Screenplay in 4 Weeks*. The ultimate purpose of this book isn't for you to become a better writer; it's for you to live a better life—to become more empowered, to experience personal enrichment and greater fulfillment in all areas.

So, while I hope you've enjoyed the writing process (and maybe picked up a few tips to help you become a better writer, if that interests you), the ultimate test of success here isn't how good a story you write, it's *how good a life you live*.

Your story might make for a compelling read—a captivating tale of an intriguing protagonist's journey into a fascinating world—yet it might not feel particularly enjoyable to *live* this story. On the other hand, your written story might not look like much—a seemingly dull tale, riddled with typos, clichés, and inconsistencies—yet it could still feel incredibly fulfilling to *be* this character and live this life.

Of course, you could also have the best of both worlds: a story that's compelling to read and fulfilling to live. But if I had to choose, I'd place far greater value on your real-life experience. That's what this whole book has been leading up to, and that's what we'll focus on in this final part: taking your new story beyond the page and actually *living* it.

During this stage of your journey, you're going to take the magnificent story you've already written (and edited and rewritten) and translate it into your beyond-the-page life. Or, to use a more apt writing metaphor, you're going to adapt your story for the "movie" of your life.

And just like a film adaptation of a novel might require some tweaking (taking into account the actors, scenery, special effects, and other film-related factors), you'll probably make adjustments during your own adaptation. You'll try out actions, attitudes, and lines of dialogue to see what works, what feels like the story you want to live, and what feels like you (the *you* that you want to be, that is—not the you who wanted to change when you started this journey). Some parts of your story might look great on the page but not work so well in your actual life, while others might make a seamless transition into the real world.

As you adapt your story for the "big screen" of your life, let's explore some key principles of screenwriting and see what inspiration and insight they can bring to your adaptation process.

Cinematography: How Does It Look?

The first step in adapting your story is to ask yourself how it might look in real life. For instance, you might know that your "lead character" is very artistic. Great! But how does this translate onto the "screen" of your life? Does it mean that she paints impressionistic landscapes? Or wears funky bohemian clothes? Or gives performance-art shows? How does her creativity manifest itself?

Or let's say you've written a new worldview for yourself: you've decided to see the world as a compassionate place, full of good, trustworthy people. How might that translate into your day-to-day life? Will you be more likely to trust strangers? Will you give people the benefit of the doubt, even when their motives seem questionable? Or will you simply feel more relaxed and have faith that it will all work out?

How might your on-the-page character translate off the page? Are there any specific scenes from your story that you know would transition easily to real life? What parts of your story might require a little more creative adaptation to work them into your daily life?

Imagine that you're a cinematographer involved in your story's adaptation (working closely with the film's writer, director, and lead actor—who are all you as well!). How would you film it to best represent this story and its lead character?

Your Adapted Self

What does the adaptation of your "character" look like? How might this new character express him- or herself in the real world? What scene or image would best capture the character's essence?

Your Adapted Story

What does the adaptation of your story look like—either in general terms or specific scenes? In what ways would it be different from your written story, or would it be basically the same?

Show and Tell

"Show, don't tell" is an oft-cited dictum for creative writers, but it's not an absolute rule. After all, there are times when it's more effective to simply tell people what you want to convey. (After all, it's called "storytelling," not "storyshowing"!) Despite the exceptions, however, "show, don't tell" is a good rule of thumb for many forms of writing—especially for screenplays. Because film is such a visual medium, you've got to be able to see the story.

Some screenwriting teachers say that a well-made movie should pass the "airplane test"—namely, if you're in an airplane that's showing a movie, but you don't buy the headphones, you should still be able to follow the story just from looking at other people's screens. That's because most effective movies show the plot through action.

The same principles apply to your real life. Your words matter; the stories you tell are important. But what matters even more is that your actions reflect the words you say, write, and think—namely, that you *show* your story rather than just telling it. Ideally, your life should be the embodiment of the principles you profess.

Keep this in mind as you adapt your story into the "movie" of your life. Think of yourself (or the "yourself" that you're in the process of creating) as the lead character of your movie, and then think of ways to bring this character's inner dynamics into their external life. For instance:

- Instead of having a character who goes around telling people, "I'm very confident," show them acting confidently.
- Instead of having a character who goes around telling people, "I'm very talented," show them in action, doing what they're talented at—and doing it very well!
- Instead of having a character who goes around telling people, "I'm very compassionate," show them helping others, listening with empathy and understanding, and acting for others' benefit.

In other words, have them not just "talk the talk" but also "walk the walk."

Of course, the writer needs to know their character's inner life very well before they can show it to others. So, review your character notes, reread your most recent story draft, and spend some time taking a good, honest look at your character's predominant qualities: confident, compassionate, or any other significant traits. And then think of how you can best express these beautiful qualities in your everyday life.

Character Traits
What are your lead character's most significant positive qualities?

Show What You Know
How can you show these qualities in your real life?

Lights, Camera...*Action!*
What actions could you take that would best embody your new character and the new story you're going to live?

Dialogue
Because your life isn't a silent movie—and words do matter—think of words that could express your new story/self in your daily life. What new "lines of dialogue" will you say? How will you say them? And, just as important, what will you *not* say? (For instance, you might decide that instead of yelling at your kids—or co-workers, partner, or others—if they do something wrong, you'll calmly share your feelings about what happened and your wishes for a more positive future. Or you might decide to say "thank you" and "I love you" more often.)

Full Creative Control

Some movie directors accept lower pay in exchange for something they value far more: full creative control. Instead of being beholden to their production company's board of directors or studio executives, these directors get the final say in how to shoot and edit their films—based on their artistic vision rather than their company's bottom line.

Just like these directors, you have full creative control over the movie of your life. No matter what story you write, who you choose to be, how you choose to live, or what you choose to do (or not do), this is *your* story! You are the writer, director, editor, and star. You write your own lines, you call the shots, make the changes, and live the scenes. No one else.

This doesn't mean you should be a solipsistic prima donna or ignore other people. In movie terms: yes, you can take into account input from others involved in the project, early viewers involved in test marketing, and even the studio executives. Just remember that, ultimately, this is *your* movie and you are answerable to yourself.

(As Rudyard Kipling wrote: "Trust yourself when all men doubt you, but make allowance for their doubting too." In terms of the RYS process, this might mean getting feedback on your story, dismissing anything that doesn't resonate, but giving special weight to any comments you receive over and over again. You can also take this approach when you receive comments about how you live your actual life—applying advice that feels right to you.)

Being the empowered, proactive author/protagonist of your own life means that you are responsible for your own story. Whether this story succeeds or flops, matches your creative vision or is a complete disaster, it's up to you. No pointing fingers. No blaming others. And no waiting for someone else to make your movie for you.

Because, above all, that's what matters: That you write your own story—in other words, that you actually live your life. And only you can do that. Nothing will get written if *you* don't write it. No one else will act your scenes for you. No one else will cut, splice, and edit it all together. It's your movie. Your story. Your life.

So, are you ready to really live it?

Taking Control

How can you claim (or reclaim) full creative control over the movie of your life? How can you take back the power and the right to direct your destiny? (For instance, do you need to rearrange your schedule to provide more freedom, stop agreeing to other people's agendas that don't fit with your own, or have a difficult-but-necessary conversation with a controlling partner or a particularly bossy boss?)

Four Steps to Implementing Your Story

So, now that you know your new story (your life-in-the-making) and your new protagonist (yourself-in-the-making), you've got a sense of how they can be adapted for the real world, and you've claimed your right to full creative control over your life, what's next? Once your inner story/movie is "greenlighted," so to speak, how do you move forward? How do you take your story beyond the page?

As writer, director, and star of your own story, you're free to take any approach that feels good to you; but if you're not sure where to start, here are four steps to help bring your story to life:

1. *Clarity* – For starters, you've got to know what you're doing. Are you attempting an entire life overhaul, or are you focusing on one specific area? (I strongly recommend that, rather than overwhelm yourself with too many changes at once, you start by picking just one particular story element to implement in your real life. But, as always, do what feels right to you.)

2. *Motivation* – So much of fiction writing comes back to character motivation. If characters don't have a very good reason to take action, they won't! (And the bigger the action, the bigger the motivation needs to be.) The same holds true in your real life: you've got to have a very good reason to change or, chances are, you won't. So, before you attempt *any* action, make sure you're motivated.

3. *Action* – This is where real-life stories diverge from on-the-page stories. With life stories, you're not just writing a story and leaving it on the page or in your mind. Once you know what you want to do and why, you actually have to *do it*.

4. *Repetition* – This is the second key distinction between written stories and life stories. Once on-the-page stories are written and edited to your satisfaction, you're done; you don't have to keep writing/editing them over and over (unless your publisher makes you, but that's a different story!). Your goal now, however, isn't just to have a good story or a single good experience but a good *life*, which means you do have to *repeatedly* live and reinforce your new story, again and again and again...until it becomes as natural as brushing your teeth every morning—or any other ingrained habit.

Take some time now to apply these steps to your own story/self/life-in-the-making.

Clarity
Pick one element of your new story that you'd like to bring to life beyond the page. Get extremely clear about precisely what it is, what it looks like, and how it will fit into your real life. (For instance, if you'd like to focus on having a positive attitude, you could focus on expressing appreciation.)

Motivation
Why is it so important for you to make this story element part of your life? (For instance, maybe your old negative attitude pushed away the people you love—and you've vowed to salvage those relationships.)

Action
What specific, concrete action will you take to bring this into your real life? (For instance, you might choose to start a gratitude list, writing down three things you appreciate before you go to bed each night.)

Repetition
Will you commit to repeating this action until it becomes a habit? When and where will you take this action, and what cues will remind you?

Make a Habit of It

Did you answer "yes" to the repetition question? If you're truly committed to making this action a habit (in other words, bringing this part of your story to life on an ongoing basis), then I'm fully committed to helping you do it. And perhaps the most important part of this is process is to convert your story into a habit—and ingrain it through repetition.

This point bears repeating: repetition is what makes the biggest difference between a written story and a real life. No matter what your story is, if you want to make it part of your ongoing life, it requires repetition and habituation. If you have an external goal, such as getting in shape, you have to create habits that lead to it—such as exercising and eating healthy foods, not just once or twice but on a regular basis. And if you have an internal goal, such as feeling happier, you don't want to feel happy only once and then say, "Yay! I've reached my goal—now I never have to feel happy again!" Of course, you want to feel happy on a regular basis, which means that you'll want to consistently do (and think and say) things that lead to happiness (such as spending more time doing what you enjoy with people you love). Repetition is how you turn your new story into your new life.

But this is easier said than done, right? How do you actually take the steps, make the changes, and ingrain the habits necessary to turn your dream story into your dream life? Every person has to find what works for them, but here are ten "Habit Helpers" that have helped me (and many others) create and maintain life-changing habits.

Ten Habit Helpers

1. *Start with Why* – There's a reason why Simon Sinek and so many other personal-growth leaders advocate this starting point, and there's a reason why I keep returning to it in this book: you need a motivation to do *anything*, you need a *big* motivation to make a big change (such as telling/living a story that's significantly different from your old one), and you need a *very* big motivation to keep repeating the change until it's a habit. So, before you take the first step in the journey of your new story/habit, make sure you know why you're taking the journey in the first place.

2. *Create Tiny Habits* – This step is inspired by B. J. Fogg, founder and director of the Stanford Behavior Design Lab and author of *Tiny Habits*. He's found that rather than focusing on your big goal (e.g., "I want to be a writer" or "I want to write a book"), it's more effective to habituate a small behavior that leads toward the goal (e.g., writing for at least ten minutes per day), using an existing behavior to "trigger" the new behavior. (On a personal note, this single step transformed my writing practice. I made the commitment that after I sit down at my writing desk each morning with my hot lemon drink [something I was already doing], I will write for at least ten minutes [the "tiny habit" I wanted to instill]. Without this tiny habit, this book might not exist!)

3. *Tell (and Live) SMART Stories* – You've probably heard of SMART goals: goals that are specific, measurable, achievable, realistic, and timed (or some similar formulation). I realize that this approach has become a cliché, but for good reason: it works! The SMART acronym is the antidote for goals and stories that are vague (e.g., "I want to improve my life"), open-ended ("I'd love to finish my book...at some point"), or unrealistic ("I want to win the Nobel Prize for Literature next year...even though I've never written anything"). If you really want to bring your story to life, be SMART about it...and use this kind of goal!

4. *Give It a Month* – You can change an attitude or a belief in an instant, but it generally takes about a month to turn that change into a habit. So, after you've selected a new behavior you want to instill, stick with it for a month. Hopefully, this is a short enough time that it doesn't feel daunting (as opposed to committing to a year...or forever!) but long enough to make it stick. As with anything new, at first it might feel awkward, uncomfortable, or downright weird. But take heart: if you do something every day, within a month it should feel as natural as brushing your teeth each morning. Soon enough, it will become part of your story, part of your life, and part of *you*. (Also, remember that committing for a month doesn't require a month of willpower; you only need a split second of discipline at the moment you're about to begin the new action—the moment when you decide whether to open your work in progress or to open Facebook, when you decide whether to wake up or hit snooze, when you decide whether to pick up the celery or the brownie. These split-second choices not only lead to your goal, they also build confidence by showing that you follow

through and keep your word—perhaps leading you to wonder: *If I did* this, *what else can I achieve?*)

5. *Stay Accountable* – Oftentimes, the single biggest factor in whether or not someone makes lasting change isn't talent, intelligence, willpower, connections, or motivation. It's simply the fact that they have an accountability partner: one person they are accountable to, tell about their commitment, and check in with on a regular basis. Even a one-line weekly email can make the shift from neglecting your dreams to *living* them!

6. *Set Yourself Up for Success* – My mother-in-law recently got a new treadmill and decided to walk on it for thirty minutes each day. This rather ambitious goal (especially considering she's in her seventies and has fibromyalgia) felt so daunting that she never used the treadmill at all. But when she scaled back to ten minutes per day, she consistently accomplished (and often surpassed) this new goal…and got into much better shape as a result. The moral here is to make your action small and simple. Better to surpass a modest (or even "laughably small") goal than to overcommit and fall short (and get stressed out and beat yourself up for "failing"). Also, set yourself up for success in terms of your schedule, support team, and environment. If you're not a morning person, don't set a goal to wake up two hours before sunrise each day and work out until noon. If you're just learning to meditate, don't start in a noisy nightclub. If you want to lose weight, join a local fitness club rather than a local cupcake club! Whatever your new story is, choose a goal that leads to it in a way that feels natural, comfortable, and fun. (After all, it's much easier to stick with an action that you actually enjoy.)

7. *Celebrate Small Wins and Interim Goals* – You don't have to reach your ultimate goal and live your ideal story before you give yourself a pat on the back. Give yourself a cheer each time you choose your new story, and reward yourself for each significant step along the way to your destination. The celebrations could include your favorite treat, a night out, or something as simple as a fist-pump accompanied by a heartfelt "woo-hoo!"

8. *Do What Works for You* – In this list, I've presented the "best practices" that have worked well for me and many others. But that doesn't mean they're the best ones for you, regardless of what "studies have shown" or the "experts" believe. Find the approach that feels right and gets results for you. This might mean trying one of the items on this list exactly as I

describe it or tweaking it to suit your style and needs. It might mean trying something different for you (which is, after all, how you get different results) or using a strategy that's already worked for you in the past. It might mean only using one approach that resonates for you or experimenting with several and then sticking with the combination that works best and feels best. This is your story and your life, so tell it and live it in your own way.

9. *Just Start* – Many strategies can get positive results, but no strategy will help you at all if you don't use it. When planning a big (or small) change, it's easy to get stuck in "ready, aim…aim!" syndrome—namely, spending so much time preparing for your journey that you never actually take it. The first step is often the hardest. Once you take that, it's easier to keep going. (Plus, you're likely to build momentum with each new step.) Also, it's easier to change directions if you're moving than to get yourself moving from a standstill. So if you're undecided about the best approach for you, just pick something—*anything*—and start it. An imperfect action is usually better than no action at all.

10. *Keep Coming Back* – Unlike written stories, lived stories aren't "one-and-done" experiences: we keep coming back to the same thoughts, words, actions, and habits—over and over. So if you're not yet experiencing the success you'd like or if you "fall off the wagon" with your new story/habit, just get up, brush yourself off, and keep coming back: back to basics, back to your Why, back to your new story, back to your habits, back to your accountability partner, back to you. And if you are experiencing great success, you still have to keep coming back. After all, your story isn't something you tell once; it's something you live daily.

After reflecting on the "habit helpers" listed above—as well as other tools and approaches you've tried (or even just heard of) for ingraining habits—answer these questions:

What's Your *Why?*

What's your reason for wanting to live your new story? Why is it so important to you? How will this reason motivate you to stick with it, even in the face of obstacles, setbacks, or challenges? What will the reward be if you're successful?

Your SMART Goal

Pick a single action—something that relates to your new story/life-in-the-making—and formulate it as a SMART goal. (E.g., instead of saying, "I want to get healthier," you might say, "I'm going to walk for at least ten minutes every day for the next month.")

Get Trigger Happy!

What existing habit will serve as your reminder/trigger to start your new habit? And what specific behavior will you perform after the trigger? (E.g., Every night after dinner, I'm going to write down three things I'm grateful for.)

Partner Up!

Who will be your accountability partner? When will you contact them and make arrangements to check in? How—and how often—will you check in (e.g., weekly emails)?

Learning from Your Past

Which habit helper(s) have you used before? Was it effective? If so, how could you apply it to your new story? If not, which other approaches (from this list or elsewhere) do you feel would work better?

Pick and Stick

Which "habit helpers" seem most appealing to you—and the most likely to work effectively? How will you implement them to help you stick with your habit and reinforce your new story?

Living the Life

In the interest of celebrating small (and large) wins, let's take a moment to reflect on what a significant milestone you've reached. After identifying your old story in Part I, releasing it in Part II, and writing a new story in Part III, you've now taken the all-important first steps to bringing that new-and-improved story to life. Just like *Harold and the Purple Crayon*, the creations of your imagination are turning into your reality! And just like the *Choose Your Own Adventure* books, you're selecting the path that feels best for you.

But once you've created a new story, brought it to life, and ingrained it through "habit helpers," what's left? Are you done with the RYS process? Almost, but not quite, because (to borrow another children's book title) you're writing a *never-ending story*. As you evolve, so will your story. The story you want to write and live today may not be the one you'll want to write and live five years (or five days) from now. Also, once you begin to live your story, you may find that it's not as appealing as you'd hoped and imagined it would be—and therefore in need of some revision in order to bring it closer to your ideal reality.

Fortunately, you already possess a tool that allows you to revise your story as you learn, grow, and continue along your life path: *editing*. Just as you edited your written story in Part III, you now get to edit your actual life! And in the next chapter, we'll explore tools that help you do exactly that.

CHAPTER TWELVE

Life Edits: Revising and Affirming Your New Story

Becoming the best version of yourself requires you to continuously edit your beliefs, and to upgrade and expand your identity.
— James Clear

U PON LEARNING that Jack Kerouac never edited his work, Truman Capote commented, "That's not writing; that's typing." Although Kerouac's style has had adherents over the years, the vast majority of professional writers fall into the Capote camp—namely, they don't publish their first drafts. Yes, they start by writing down their initial ideas and impulses, but then they read what they've written and revise it (usually many times) until they arrive at a version that, as closely as possible, matches their highest vision.

This is the approach you took while writing your own story: You didn't just write it once; you started by taking notes, then you wrote a first draft, then you edited it, then you rewrote it, then you edited some more…and so on, until you got it just right. Because that's how masterpieces get (re)written.

There's a reason why this book isn't called *Write Your Story*! Editing and rewriting are important parts of creating a written story or a life-story. The ability to edit gives us the power to change—to transform not only our written stories but also our real lives. Editing gives us the freedom to explore and experiment, grow and evolve, learn from trial and error, and make adjustments that lead to a happier, healthier, more fulfilling life. Being willing and able to edit our story means that we're not stuck with our first draft (literally or figuratively) simply because "that's the way it's written."

You might want to edit a written story to correct a mistake or fill in a missing piece. Or you might just want to make it better—more exciting, interesting, and fulfilling. The same is true as you edit your life: you might want to fix mistakes, add new ideas, or take what's already okay and make it exceptional. You might make changes because you realize that an idea that looked good on paper doesn't translate into real life. Or you might simply get new ideas and new desires as you continue to live, learn, and evolve—in which case, you'll want to revise your story and your life to bring them closer to your new ideals.

Throughout this chapter, we'll explore tools for fine-tuning your story for the real world so that you can tweak, hone, and polish until not just your story but your entire life becomes a masterpiece.

In some ways, this process will be similar to editing written work. No, we won't worry about grammar, spelling, or punctuation, but we will look to create a life-story that's engaging and fulfilling—one that expresses your highest vision for yourself.

In other ways, however, editing life is different from editing writing. For instance, if I had to summarize the goal of editing writing in just one word, I'd say *readability*. (*Effective* and *engaging* would be close runners-up, since you want writing to engage the reader and effectively convey the writer's story or message.) For life editing, however, the one-word key is *alignment*.

Edit Your Life into Alignment

Imagine you're playing a tug of war, and you have five people on your team. One of them is pulling the rope forward, one is pulling backward, the third person is pulling to the side, and the other two aren't pulling at all. It's going to make it very hard to win the game, right?

If you could suggest a new strategy, I'm guessing it would be: *let's all pull in the same direction!*

The same is true for your words, actions, character, story, and life. To be effective, they need to work in alignment as a team. For instance, if you write a new story about how intelligent you are, but then you constantly talk about how stupid you are (even "jokingly"—like our friend Nars), it's going to erode your story's strength and your self-esteem.

Fortunately, however, you have the proverbial red pen, and you can edit any disempowering words right out of your life and replace them with words that align with your highest character and story.

This doesn't mean you have to constantly "correct" yourself while you're in the middle of saying, doing, or even thinking something that might not be the perfect embodiment of your highest story/self/life. As I've mentioned, most authors don't edit while they're writing—it would be counterproductive, like two tug-of-war partners pulling in different directions. Likewise, you don't need to "edit" your life while you're living it. However, you can train yourself to become more aware of the actions you take and the words you use and gradually create a habit of choosing ones that align better with your new story.

You can do this in lots of ways. With your words, for instance, you can reread emails before you send them—and remove/replace anything that undermines your new story. Or if you say something disempowering during a conversation, you can say, "Let me rephrase that..." and then rephrase it! And if you notice recurring thoughts that run counter to your new story, you can repeat an affirmation—or perhaps the summary of your new story.

Only you can know what feels like the right practices and the right alignment for you, but here are some general guidelines and suggestions for words you might want to edit:

- *Self-deprecating words/phrases* – such as "I'm not a rocket scientist," sarcastically referring to yourself as "Einstein," or even a simple "Duh" in response to a mental lapse.

- *Words that imply desperation or scarcity* – including a lack of love, money, or time (e.g., "There just aren't enough hours in the day" or "I *need* more money...*now!*")

- *Questions with disempowering presuppositions* – namely, questions based on negative assumptions, such as, "Why is everyone so mean to me?" No matter how you answer, you've bought into the premise that everyone *is* mean to you (which I guarantee is not true—and is certainly not aligned with your highest self/story).

- *"Red-flag" words, such as "obviously," "of course," or "never"* – No, they're not always bad for you, but when you hear them come out of your mouth, put up your RYS antennae because there's a good chance that some disempowering words are in the vicinity. (E.g., "*Of course* the party is on the one day I have to work" or "I *never* finish on time.")

- *Unhealthy metaphors* – or any figures of speech that imply a worldview not aligned with your new story. For instance, if your new story is that your business flows naturally and pleasurably for you, you'll probably want to edit out sayings like "It's a dog-eat-dog world," or "It's a jungle out there."

- *Words that demean what you want (or those who already have it)* – For instance, if you'd like to work less (or not have to work at all if you don't want to) and you meet someone who's arranged their life to make this possible, you might sarcastically say, "Well, *that* must be nice, only having to work one day a week—poor baby!" Yes, actually, it *is* nice! But a sour-grapes attitude isn't going to attract it to you. So, why not celebrate this accomplishment, by saying something such as, "That's wonderful! I'm also consciously working toward a similar goal."

- *Sarcasm* – Period.

- *"I am…" followed by anything you don't want to be* – The words "I am" carry a tremendous power—the power of self-identification. So make sure that whatever words follow "I am" embody the identity/character that you want to be.

If you're not sure which words to edit out of your story, here's a simple test: ask yourself, *Do I want them to be true?* If the answer is no, they've got to go!

Another editing game you can play is to mentally insert the phrase "if you say so" after statements. For instance:

- It's a jungle out there…if you say so!
- Relationships are hard work…if you say so!
- The body is fragile…if you say so!
- Things tend to work out for the best…if you say so!

If you think of stories, beliefs, and expectations as self-fulfilling prophecies (which I do), which ones would you want to fulfill? Which ones would you want to come true? Which ones would you want to reinforce?

For me, the last statement in this bullet list sounds good. It's in alignment with my highest good and my best story. The other three…not so much. So if I ever notice myself writing, saying, or thinking these things, I'll remember to edit them—and replace them with statements that I want to be true, such as "Business flows naturally, relationships are a joy, and my body is becoming increasingly strong and healthy." Now *those* are stories I can gladly reinforce!

Aligning Your Story and Your Life

What parts of your current life (including your words, actions, or thoughts) aren't aligned with your new story (in other words, with your life goals and the person you want to be)? What changes could you make to bring everything into alignment with your highest goals, values, and desires?

Deletions

What words or actions would you like to delete from your life (e.g., procrastination, self-deprecating humor, or words of scarcity)?

Additions

What words would you like to add to your life? What words or actions would more accurately reflect the story you want to tell and live?

Editing Subplots

So far, you may be thinking of editing in terms of making major changes in the most significant areas of your life. And this is definitely a good place to start the editing process. After all, just like any good fiction writer, you don't want to leave gaping holes in your main story.

But you also want to be successful (and joyful and fulfilled) in areas that aren't your primary focus—hobbies, side interests, and other small-but-still-important activities. As with fiction, you can edit not only your primary story but also the subplots of your life. This is what my wife did several years ago when she found that changing one simple word changed her entire outlook—an amazing shift that also reminded us of the power of the stories we tell ourselves.

At the time, most of our "A" story was going more or less the way we wanted. On a personal level, we'd arranged our lives so we could spend most of our time together, which has always been our top priority. Professionally, we'd recently turned a corner—after years of hustling and struggling to make ends meet, our work-from-home business was finally starting to thrive. And creatively, we were both focused on doing what we love: writing books that nourished our souls and helped others live their best lives. However, there was one area of her own life that was a long way from what she wanted: her health.

Although we try to maintain a healthy lifestyle—eating well and enjoying healthful activities such as kayaking and walking on the beach—admittedly, health has never been a primary focus for us...unless something goes wrong, as it did a few years ago. Apparently, Jodi's adrenal glands had had enough of all the stressful hustling, and they decided to do something about it: they went on strike. Jodi learned of this decision one morning when, like the woman on the LifeCall commercial, she fell and couldn't get up. For many months afterward, she was barely able to stand up or walk, stay awake for more than a few hours at a time, or work at anywhere close to the level she'd been keeping up for years.

Nearly as frustrating as the newly imposed physical restrictions was the story Jodi kept repeating: "My body is my enemy." This story made perfect sense to her. After all, she had big plans for work, writing, and living her life to the fullest, but her body simply wouldn't cooperate. It was literally keeping her down, like a hostile force, sabotaging her deepest desires.

As the months wore on, she repeated this story—aloud to me and, far more often, silently to herself. And each passing day reinforced and justified telling this story. She eventually realized, however, that this story wasn't serving her—it was actually making her feel worse. And she started to wonder if there was a more helpful way to look at her experience. *What if my body is trying to help me? What if it's sending me important messages? What if it's not an enemy at all but actually a friend?* So, she decided to edit one word of her old story: "My body is my enemy" became "My body is my friend."

No, her body didn't miraculously heal overnight as soon as she adopted this new story. (In fact, although she's improved tremendously, she's still not back to the optimal health she wants.) But her story about her condition did change her *experience* of it. From this new perspective, she saw that her newly imposed physical limitations were actually guiding her closer to a more authentic, desirable life: one filled with balance, calm, and lots of downtime for quiet reflection and healing. She saw her body as a teammate, encouraging her to do what was in her best interest (primarily, rest). She saw it as a messenger, reminding her of what she already knew on a deeper level—messages she'd ignored for years…until she no longer could. She saw it as a friend that only wanted the best for her and helped her to get it, even if it meant taking an unexpected approach.

How about you? Are there any secondary areas of your life that you'd like to change? Take some time now to reflect on the subplots in your life—areas that aren't your primary focus but are still important. Then think of how you might edit those areas to bring you greater joy, fulfillment, and alignment with the rest of your new story and the new life you're creating based on it.

Secondary but Significant

What areas of your life aren't your primary focus but are nonetheless important to you (e.g., your health, hobbies, or casual friendships)?

Editing Your Subplots

Which of these secondary areas would you most like to edit? What changes would you like to make? Do you want a major overhaul in any of these areas or just a few minor tweaks? What would you like to eliminate altogether? What new words or actions would you like to add to these areas of your life?

Building on the Positive

In this book, we spend a lot of time addressing negative stories—exposing their detrimental effects and also exploring how they can be changed for the better. However, it's important to note that not all the stories we hear in our youth (and throughout our lives) are harmful. In fact, some of them are wonderfully supportive, nourishing, and empowering—and can lead us into a glorious future. But this doesn't mean that we can't also "edit" these stories—and the lives that reflect them—to make them even more glorious.

One example of a positive story that grew even more positive results comes from "Saint Kath." No, she's not a literal saint—at least she doesn't see herself that way (although her family does—they're the ones who gave her the nickname). Kath simply sees herself as someone who sees the good in people and situations, practices patience (a virtue she attributes to often being placed in situations that require a lot of it), and treats others the way she would want to be treated. People who know her say that she's an advocate for her family and friends, someone who is there for them in a quiet way, even during times that aren't so fun. And they all agree that she's someone who's able to see the blessings in everyday experiences.

So, where did this positive outlook originate? With positive stories! As a youngster, Kath was told that she was loved. She learned that, no matter how things look at times, the world can be a loving place. She also learned that you can "polish a coal into a diamond"—namely, that even difficult situations contain lessons and blessings.

As an adult, she continues to take these stories to heart, even when life isn't going her way. For example, with her positive outlook on life, even a broken washing machine presents an opportunity to count her blessings: she has a car (blessing), she lives near a laundromat (blessing), and she has enough quarters for the machines (blessing).

Yes, difficult situations sometimes annoy her at first, but she's able to look back at her life and reinforce the story that even challenges contain blessings—a story that grew out of a seed of love.

Like Kath, we can edit even very positive stories to make our own lives even more positive. One of the most effective ways to do this is to change the way we respond to our circumstances, learning to interpret them in ways that best support us. No, you can't always control other people and situations, but you can control how you see them and how you respond. With a bit of conscientious "life editing," you can learn to polish the "coal" you encounter until it shines like a diamond. And then you can polish the diamonds, too!

Polishing the Diamonds

How can you build on the positives in your life? (For instance, you could spend even more time connecting with loved ones, visiting your favorite places, or engaging in a hobby that brings you joy.)

Editing Your Responses

How could you respond more positively to your life circumstances (whatever they may be)? This might include viewing things in a different light, taking different actions in response to externals that are beyond your control, or sometimes choosing *not* to respond (rather than being reactive and getting sucked into a situation you'd rather not get involved with).

Affirming Your New Life-Story

Whether you're editing out the negatives in your life or building on the positives, it takes practice to change the way you live. Forming new habits requires repetition. This is true whether these habits are actions, thoughts, or emotions.

Just like you have certain things you do every day (such as taking a shower and brushing your teeth), you have many habitual thoughts—mental loops you've played so often that if your brain were a record, you would've worn out the grooves (especially if you've been playing these loops ever since the days of vinyl records)! The same idea is true for long-standing emotional habits. Maybe you've been reacting to certain triggers the same way for so many years that you don't even consider alternatives. (For instance, you might always get irritated when you're stuck in traffic or waiting in long lines.) Or maybe you tend to return to the same habitual emotion under many circumstances. (Most people have a "go-to" emotion, habitually returning to anger, fear, or sadness.)

Chances are, you've been reinforcing your habitual actions, thoughts, and emotions for years. Yes, you may have just written your story for the first time just a few days ago (or, if you're an extremely fast reader, hours ago), but I can guarantee you've been living it since long before then. Fortunately, no matter how long-standing your habits may be, they can be changed. It just takes some repetition. But what exactly are you supposed to repeat?

With a new action, it's pretty clear what you're supposed to do. (For example, if you're forming the habit of exercising or meditating, just do those things.) But how do you habituate a new thought or emotion you'd like to add to your life-story?

One of the most direct ways is by using affirmations—words or phrases that embody the new story you'd like to ingrain and live. (You can think of affirmations as short aspirational stories—namely, stories of what you aspire to experience in your real life.) You've got a head start in this area because you've already created your affirmations by writing and editing your new story and by answering the questions earlier in this chapter. Let's revisit what you've already written, make any helpful changes, and then use this as the basis for a new affirmation.

Adding Affirmations

Revisit your response to the "Additions" exercise ("What words would you like to add to your life? What words or actions would more accurately reflect the story you want to tell and live?"). Then pick one word or phrase from this response (or something else from your new story or something new you come up with right now) that seems most powerful or important to you right now—one that reflects your ideal story and self. Rewrite it in a way that's concise, easy to remember, and easy to repeat.

Post It

Write your affirmation on three separate sticky notes and stick them in conspicuous places (e.g., on your refrigerator, near your workspace, in your wallet, on your bathroom mirror—any place where you'll see them often).

Affirmation Habituation

The point of an affirmation isn't just to write it a few times and then forget about it; you want to turn it into a habit. With this in mind, create affirmation triggers (e.g., say it every time you open the refrigerator, which is easy to remember if you've posted your affirmation on the refrigerator door). Also, commit to saying it many times each day for the next month. Before too long, the new words, thoughts, and emotions—and the story that goes with them—should be a natural part of your everyday life. What affirmation trigger will you use to turn your words into reality?

Affirmation Alternatives: Bridges, Questions, and Evidence

Countless people have been helped by affirmations, which is why I can heartily recommend them as an effective tool for changing your life story. I have to admit, however, that I sometimes feel resistance to using them. What often happens with me is that I'll say an affirmation, and then part of my brain will immediately start to refute the statement. For instance, if I say, "I'm always punctual," another part of my brain might respond with, "No you're not—you're frequently late!" If I step up the affirmation (e.g., "I am the *epitome* of punctuality!"), it might just strengthen my mental rebuttal: "Okay, now you're just flat-out lying!"

I know that the point of an affirmation is to repeat it until you believe it, internalize it, and live it—so that it's *not* a lie. But when I've tried the "fake it till you make it" approach, I haven't often reached the second part.

Like I said, this is not a knock against affirmations. They do work. And I have used them effectively on occasion. But I've generally gotten better results when I put my own twist on them, using these alternative approaches, which might work better for you, too.

Bridges

When I want to reach a goal that feels unrealistically out of reach, I sometimes use what I call "bridge affirmations." These are interim truths. For instance, if you're a beginning musician, you might aspire to play like a master; however, you probably wouldn't believe an affirmation such as "I'm a master of my instrument!" But you could believe "I'm steadily improving my musical abilities" or "I'm moving toward musical mastery."

As in these examples, bridge affirmations are often phrased as progressives (*-ing* verbs, such as *improving* and *moving*), focusing on progress, process, and the direction you're facing and moving in—as opposed to pretending you've already reached the ultimate goal.

If you find yourself put off by affirmations that feel inauthentically positive, you might be glad to know that you can create bridge affirmations from negative sentences! You can turn around even the most discouraging thought simply by adding one little word after it: *yet*. For instance, the final word of "I'm not close to my goal...*yet*" makes the difference between despair and hope. That one little word adds the assumption that you *will* be close to your goal at some point—you're just not there *yet*. Then you can follow up the revised sentence with a believably hopeful statement. For instance, "I'm not close to my goal" could become "I'm not close to my goal yet, but I'll take steps forward until I *am* close to my goal—and I'll keep going until I reach it!"

What I like about bridge affirmations is that I can really believe them. I don't have to play any mental games or go through linguistic contortions. My only caveat with bridge affirmations is that you don't get stuck on the bridge! Namely, don't get so accustomed to moving *toward* your goals that you never reach them. Just like an actual bridge is intended to take you from where you are to the opposite shore, an affirmation is intended to make your ultimate goal a present-time reality, not just a distant dream.

With this in mind, you can combine bridge affirmations with standard "as-if" affirmations (stated in present tense as if you're already living your ideal story). For instance, if your goal is to reach your ideal weight but you resist saying "I'm at my ideal weight," you might combine that with a bridge, such as, "I'm moving consistently toward my ideal weight." Or, for a writing goal, you might say, "I'm making steady progress while completing my novel." Or you could use this method for an inner goal such as, "Joy is becoming a bigger and bigger part of my life." You could also use a bridge affirmation until you get within striking distance of your goal and then switch to an "as-if" affirmation.

There are many ways to create and work with affirmations. The key is to find the fit for you—something you can believe, repeat, and make real in your life.

Your Bridge Affirmation
Whether or not you believe your ultimate goal/story/affirmation (yet), you can probably come up with something believable and effective that moves you in that direction. What bridge affirmation might work for you?

Your Combined Affirmation
If you combined your bridge affirmation with your ultimate-goal affirmation, what would the combined affirmation be?

Affirmative Questions: "Leading the Witness"

So far, the affirmations we've considered have all been statements, but affirmations can also take the form of questions. In fact, these are my favorite kinds, because they open doors, stimulate creativity, and lead you toward your chosen goals and ideal life-story.

Some of my favorite "affirmative questions" are those that begin with "What if...":

- What if things go smoothly today?
- What if I have a creative breakthrough?
- What if I were more productive than usual today?
- What if I could lean into my story a bit more?
- What if I could live my story?

What-if questions can be tailored to almost any situation—general or specific. Even if you don't come up with an answer right away, they at least get you looking for answers—which changes your focus, the direction you're facing, and your expectations.

They're also a great way to turn around discouragement. For instance, if you find yourself thinking, "I'm never going to reach my goal," you could ask: "But what if I could?" Or if you're feeling upset, you could ask, "What if I felt happy?" And if a question like this feels like too big of a leap from your current state, you could use the "bridge" approach and ask something like, "What if I could start to feel even a little bit better?"

Many writers begin creative works by asking a what-if question, which often serves as a writing prompt that can lead to an entire full-length work. (These questions are similar to the "Magic If" in Konstantin Stanislavski's acting method, in which actors ask themselves what-if questions that reveal more about the characters they play.) You can do something similar in your actual life—except instead of just *writing* your answers, you can *live* them!

What-if questions aren't the only ones that can shift you into a more positive frame of mind. You can turn almost any affirmation into a question, as long as it has a positive presupposition—that is, as long as it's based on a positive premise and is likely to lead to positive answers. For instance:

- Why am I starting to feel better? (The presupposition here is: I *am* starting to feel better.)

- How can I accomplish this? (The presupposition is: I *can* accomplish this.)

- What are some effective methods for reaching my goal? (The multi-part presupposition is that I *can* and *will* reach my goal, and that there are numerous ways to do it—it's just a matter of finding the most *effective* ones.)

One of my favorites questions is, "How can I afford this?"—which (as Robert Kiyosaki points out in *Rich Dad, Poor Dad*) not only assumes you *can* afford this (it's just a matter of *how*) but also gets your mental wheels turning for creative solutions to this problem. Whereas statements such as "I can't afford this" or even yes/no questions such as "Can I afford this?" stop mental/creative activity (the conversation is over within a syllable!), an open-ended question stimulates the mind. And when you give your mind a stimulating question, it's likely to find an answer—oftentimes, many!

If you've ever been involved in a court case—or even just watched or read courtroom dramas—you've probably heard objections raised when a lawyer asks a question that is "leading the witness." In trials, a question such as "Why did you commit this crime?" presupposes that they *did* commit the crime. But leading questions also have a positive use outside the courtroom: they can lead you to assume that reaching your goals is possible, that feeling better is possible, and that you're already in the process of living your aspirational story.

So, if you'd like to lead yourself (gently and lovingly) toward the story you want to live, come up with your own affirmative questions…and then answer them and live them!

Your Affirmative Questions

What questions might stimulate your creativity and get your mental wheels moving in a positive direction? You can use what-if questions or any other questions based on positive presuppositions—namely, leading questions that lead you in the direction you want to go. (Hint: If you're not sure what to ask, you can always rephrase your affirmations as questions. For instance, if your affirmation is, "I am healthy" or "I am getting healthier all the time," you could ask yourself, "Why am I feeling so much healthier?" or "How can I keep improving my health?")

Mountains of Evidence

As effective as affirmations and stimulating questions may be, I've found that nothing boosts confidence like evidence of past success.

When I set the goal of writing this book, I had several options: I could have simply pumped myself up with positive affirmations ("I can finish this book!") or empowering questions ("What's the best way for me to finish this book?"). But the approach that gave me the most confidence was to simply remind myself that I've already written numerous books. I've done it before, so I can— and *will*—do it again.

The same holds true for any goals—even internal ones, such as wanting to feel good: You've felt good before, so you can (and will) feel good again.

No matter what story you'd like to live, there's almost certainly some evidence that can support you in reaching your goal. Most likely, there's a "mountain of evidence" (as lawyers often say). The trick is to rummage through your mental files of memories to find evidence that supports you (rather than replaying old disempowering stories that work against you).

Let's return to our story-writing, film-adaptation, and editing metaphors: Imagine you've got a mountain of pre-written and pre-filmed material. Now you get to play the role of editor: you sift through the "cutting-room floor" and find lots of material. Some of it might support your highest vision, some of it might detract from it, and a lot of it is totally unrelated. The key is to find the material that boosts you up. Create a "greatest hits" compilation instead of a blooper reel!

You've got millions of moments to choose from—surely you can find *something* that supports you and your goals. Think you can't? Well, what if you could? And if you were able to find supportive evidence, what might it be? (If you picked up on my not-so-subtle affirmative questions, good—you're a fast learner!) Now, let's put that evidence to good use: supporting your new story.

Exhibit A (and B, C, D, and Beyond)

What memories, experiences, and evidence from your past would support you and the new story/character you're currently creating? Write down all the possibilities you can think of, and then circle the ones that are most empowering.

Ladies and Gentlemen of the Jury...

How could you present your strongest pieces of evidence (the ones you circled in the previous exercise) to an inner jury to prove beyond a reasonable doubt that you can and will reach your goals and live the life you desire?

Reframing Revisited

As a final tool for editing and affirming the story you want to live, let's revisit the idea of reframing—in other words, presenting your story in a different light or putting it into a new frame of reference. This is so important when choosing supportive evidence because it's not so much *what* you've experienced that counts here, but how you *frame* those experiences—how you interpret them—that makes the difference. In other words, what matters here is the story you tell yourself *about* your experiences.

Maybe you've been telling yourself a disempowering story that could be turned into confidence-boosting evidence simply by changing your perspective. Maybe that "humiliating" experience is actually kind of funny in retrospect. Maybe it could teach you not to take yourself so seriously. Or maybe it could remind you that if you lived through that awful time, you can get through anything. What great lessons! What great evidence of your strength, your humor, your resilience, and your character!

And if that's what you can do with your *worst* memories, just think of what you can do with your *best*! (In fact, don't just think about it—write about it.)

Reframing the Blooper Reel

Think of a story you've retold (to others or even just to yourself) that drags you down; then reframe it in the most positive, empowering light possible.

Reframing the Highlight Reel

Now think of stories and experiences that are already wonderful and reframe them to make them even more empowering—focusing especially on aspects that could support you in your current goals and your new story.

Life Edits in Action: Seven Steps to a New-and-Improved "Draft"

So, how do you put all these elements together, implement these tools, and actually make the changes you want in your everyday life? What does the process of "editing your life" look like in action?

You'll most likely want to personalize an approach that feels right and works well for you—picking and choosing from the strategies I've presented or techniques that have worked for you (or others) in the past—but these seven steps can serve as general guidelines for your life-editing process:

1. *Observe Your Life* – Notice what's going on inside you and in your external life. What's working effectively? Where are you getting (or not getting) the results you want? What are your most common thoughts and emotions? What would you like more of or less of? What do you want to stay the same, and what would you like to change?

2. *Choose Your Focus* – Pick one area you'd like to "edit." Do you want to change something that's not quite the way you'd like it to be, add something completely new, or eliminate something altogether?

3. *Set Your Intention* – What's your goal? What does your post-edit "scene of success" look like and feel like?

4. *Trigger Your Behavior* – Pick a new action that leads to your intended goal and perform that action after something you already do (e.g., after I brush my teeth each morning, I'll meditate). Perform the action consistently for one month but give yourself the flexibility to make adjustments that serve you best. For instance, if you set an intention to do twenty-five push-ups after breakfast but have trouble making it to ten, you might want to start with just one or two and gradually add more as your strength grows. (Note: Even if you'd like to eliminate something or are focused on an internal goal, it's still helpful to add an external behavior. For instance, you could meditate to reduce stress.)

5. *Build Your Affirmations* – Just as you might build your actions over time (e.g., doing more push-ups as you get stronger), you can build affirmations that reflect your growing confidence. You might start with something as basic as "change is possible" (perhaps mentally citing examples when you or others changed). From there, you might ask

leading questions, such as, "What if I *could* make this positive change?"—or reframe past experiences, such as, "What if those past setbacks or 'failures' taught me valuable lessons that will assist in my future success?" When you feel ready, you could transition to bridge affirmations (such as "I'm making progress toward my goal") and then, when your goal is within sight or feels believable, you could use as-is affirmations (such as "It feels great to experience this success"). During this process, you'll be like "The Little Engine That Could," transitioning from "I think I can" to "I *know* I can"!

6. *Celebrate Your Evidence* – As you reach your goals, you're building a "mountain of evidence" of your ability to write the story and create the life you want. But you don't need to wait until you've reached a huge goal or built a "mountain" in order to celebrate. In fact, celebrating small wins, interim goals, and mini-successes is one of the best ways to keep you inspired and moving toward larger goals. So, reward yourself (in healthy ways that feel good) for each mini-milestone you reach, and take a few moments to cheer yourself on after *every* action you take toward your new and improved life-story.

7. *Repeat Your Success* – Once you've written and edited a book to your satisfaction, you don't need to keep rewriting it. With a life story, however, repetition is essential. With an inner goal such as feeling relaxed, for instance, you don't want to feel relaxed just once and then go back to being stressed out; you want to feel consistently relaxed, which means you have to repeat the thoughts and actions that lead to relaxation. With an outer goal, such as achieving a healthy weight, you don't want to reach your ideal weight and then gain everything back; you want to repeat the actions (and thoughts) that help you maintain your healthy weight. And just like you can adjust your affirmations or your behaviors, you can always revise your approach to optimize your success or better reflect your changing priorities.

As I mentioned, you can use this life-editing process for external goals (such as writing a book) or inner intentions (such as feeling more relaxed). With the book-writing example, for instance, the process might look something like this:

You observe your life and see that you generally feel good and are reaching (or moving toward) your most important goals…with one notable exception:

you're not making progress on the book you've been meaning to write. So you choose to focus on this area and set the intention to finish your book this year. To move toward this goal, you decide to write for at least ten minutes a day after you get dressed each morning. You tell yourself, "It feels great to be making steady progress on my book," and you celebrate successes, large and small: each time you complete a writing session, you pump your fist in the air and say, "Awesome!" (B. J. Fogg's suggestion, which I use daily!); each time you finish writing a chapter, you go out for dinner at your favorite restaurant; and when you complete the manuscript, you take a week-long vacation. But you don't stop there; because you want to be a lifelong writer, you keep up your writing habit, expanding your daily goal to twenty minutes but taking off weekends in order to spend more time with your family.

And although it might seem harder to implement this process for inner goals (which can sometimes feel vague or unquantifiable), you can go through the exact same process. For instance, let's say you observe your life and notice that although you're reaching many external goals, you feel much more stress than you'd like, so you choose to focus on editing this part of your life. If you'd currently rate your stress level at an 8 out of 10, you could set the intention to reduce this to a 3 (or lower). To this end, you decide to meditate for at least ten minutes every morning after you brush your teeth. You supplement this practice with positive affirmations, starting with basics (e.g., "I've felt relaxed before, so I know I can feel more relaxed again"), moving on to leading questions (e.g., "What would it feel like to be more relaxed?" or "How can I experience even deeper relaxation?") and bridge affirmations (e.g., "It's such a relief to be leaning into ever-deepening relaxation"), and finally shifting to as-if affirmations when you reach (or get close to) your goal of decreasing your stress level to 3 or below (e.g., "I love my new relaxed life!").

As I mentioned, feel free to adjust this process to suit your needs. You may want to incorporate techniques that have worked for you in other areas, such as using hypnosis or EFT (Emotional Freedom Technique) tapping to "edit out" unwanted habits. You might check in regularly with an accountability partner to help you stay on track. Or you might find that just one or two of these steps (e.g., actions and affirmations) are enough to create the results you want. Whatever approach you take, what matters most is that it feels right for you…and actually works!

Edit Your Life in 7 Steps

Consider how you might be able to use this process in your own life...

Observe Your Life

As you reflect on your inner and outer life, what areas might you want to "edit" in some way?

Choose Your Focus

Which of these areas would you most like to change? How? Would you like to make minor adjustments to something that's not as positive as you'd like, eliminate a bad habit, or add something new?

Set Your Intention

What's your goal for this process? What would you like your life to look like and feel like once you've finished editing?

Trigger Your Behavior

What new action will you take to lead you toward your goal? What existing behavior (e.g., brushing your teeth, eating dinner, or coming home from work) will trigger the new behavior?

Build Your Affirmations

What affirmations could support you throughout this process? (Remember that you can use different types, including bridge affirmations, leading questions, and as-if affirmations.)

Celebrate Your Evidence

How will you celebrate your small, medium, and large wins? (For instance, you could do a "happy dance" each time you perform your new behavior.)

Repeat Your Success

What can you do to make sure that your success is not a one-time fluke but an ongoing part of your new life? What can you change (if it's not working as well as you'd like) or reinforce (if it is working well) to set yourself up for long-term success?

What Else?

Are there any other tools, resources, or approaches—not already mentioned in this seven-step process—that might help you edit your life effectively? Is there something you've used successfully in other areas that you could apply to this new focus? Is there something you've heard of or seen others using effectively that you'd like to try for yourself?

Preparing for Your Final Exam

Now you've got all the tools you need to write a great story, adapt it into your real life, and continually update and improve it. So, if all goes smoothly, you should be set for life.

But "if all goes smoothly" is a pretty big "if"! Just when we think we've got everything under control, life has a way of throwing a wrench in our best-laid plans.

However, because you have the power to reframe your experiences, you can choose how you see these "wrenches": are they evidence that the universe doesn't want you to be happy, are they valuable pieces of feedback, or are they tests that you're now capable of passing with flying colors?

In the final chapter, we'll explore the latter possibilities, learning how to grow from life's feedback and ace whatever tests may come your way.

CHAPTER THIRTEEN

Reality Check:
The Workshop of Life

You are the author of your own life story. You have the leading role and get to determine how you interact with your supporting cast and other characters. Without realizing it, you may have allowed the events in your life to write your story for you rather than taking deliberate action to write it in your own voice. What will it take to love your life story to create the happy endings you desire?
— Susan C. Young

MANY STEPS IN THIS BOOK are designed to be taken on your own. To write and edit a story, all you need are writing materials and your private thoughts and emotions. The story you create is between you and yourself.

There comes a time, however, when your story needs to reach beyond yourself—to get out of your head, off the page, and into the world. Not only is this your goal (to *live* your story), but it's also a way to get incredibly valuable feedback—through a real-world reality check.

In terms of the writing process, this experience is a bit like having your story workshopped. Most creative-writing programs are centered around workshops where you share your writing with your classmates and get their feedback. Sometimes workshops are extremely encouraging—people love your work and can't wait for the next installment. At other times, they can be discouraging—what you'd hope to convey didn't get across at all. But in either case, it's helpful because it gets your story out of your head and into the world. And you get a reality check.

The point of workshops isn't to judge your work as "good" or "bad" (although, in workshops and in life, you'll sometimes encounter self-appointed arbiters of quality). The point is to see how effectively you're communicating your intentions. After all, effective writing is about effective communication, so if what you want to communicate isn't getting across to the reader, you may have to rethink your approach.

In the RYS process, you also have a workshop—a place where you can get your story out of your head and into the world, receive feedback, see if your story is working the way you intended, and think of ways that it might be improved. This workshop is *your life!*

In your daily life, you find out whether your story is "working"—is it living up to your hopes, or could it use some revision? Just like a fiction workshop, you'll get clear feedback about which parts are strong, which parts are weak, and which parts need to go altogether. And all of this is helpful because all of it can strengthen your story and your life.

For instance, let's say your new story stars a healthy, confident "protagonist" (the new you), so you find ways to exhibit confidence (e.g., speaking in public) and get healthier (e.g., joining a gym, cooking/eating healthier meals, or practicing stress-reduction techniques). And as you incorporate these elements of your character and story into your daily life, you'll receive feedback. Some of it will come from the outside (e.g., people clapping after your speech or telling you how healthy you look), but much of it will come from within. For instance, your body might tell you, "I don't like this new workout regimen!" Or your taste buds might tell you, "The new meal is pretty good, but go a bit easier on the salt next time." Or your emotions might say, "I *love* that relaxing meditation—let's do more of that!"

As with a fiction-writing workshop, however, you don't have to take every suggestion you receive. You get to decide which suggestions to dismiss and which ones might actually help you improve your story. But how do you decide?

Whenever you receive feedback—from other people or from your own inner reactions—the key question to ask yourself is: *Does it resonate?* You'll know which suggestions strike a chord with you and which ones seem way off base. The ones that resonate usually feel like a light shining on something you were already thinking or feeling but hadn't quite put into words before. Or they might raise a lot of energy—positive (agreement) or negative (vehement resistance). The feedback that doesn't resonate probably won't register much at all, one way or the other. If you're not sure about a piece of feedback, you can always just sit with it for a while before making any decisions about whether or not to incorporate it into your life-story.

For example, if your body complains about your new workouts, saying something like, "All this jogging makes me ache. Let's just go back to the way we used to do it—sleeping in and eating whatever we want," you can either accept this suggestion, reject it outright, or just sit with it for a while. You might tell your complaining body, "Let's just give the workouts a month. Who knows, you might come to like them. And if not, we can think about revising them to make them more enjoyable."

Of course, your body might have very valuable feedback. Even a "complaint" might raise a valid point. For instance, you might realize you're pushing yourself too hard and you need to ease into your new workouts more slowly in order to avoid injuries. Or you might realize that this is merely the resurfacing of an old, outdated story—the voice of self-sabotaging habits that no longer serve you (if they ever did).

If you're in touch with your true self, you can be strong enough to consider others' viewpoints, even if they differ from your own. In fact, this is often the kind of feedback that can help you the most by broadening your perspective. Of course, you can also benefit tremendously from positive reinforcement, especially when you're taking the first steps of living a new story (a time when you might feel particularly fragile and in need of a kind word or two).

Regardless of the feedback you get, however, *you* get to decide whether it's in alignment with your highest self, the story you want to write/live, and your overall best interests. And only you get to decide whether or not you want to incorporate it into your life. Because, after all, it's *your* story and *your* life.

Feedback

What feedback have you gotten—from yourself or from others—when you've shared parts of your new character and new story with the world? Does it resonate? If so, how might you be able to use it to help you strengthen your story/character in the future?

The Company You Keep

Rewriting your story can be a complex process even when you're all alone. You sort through thoughts, emotions, memories, dreams, desires, and other inner experiences. You write, edit, rewrite, and adapt your story to fit into the real world. And then you get feedback from your thoughts, emotions, and body about how your story is working out. And then you go back to the page, rewrite your story, incorporate those revisions into your real life, and continue the process.

Wow! There's a lot going on, isn't there?

But this process becomes even more complex when you factor in other people. Yes, many people will support you during this process: your true friends, your accountability partner, understanding peers, online communities, and others in your support system. Sometimes all you need is one person who truly sees you, respects your journey, and appreciates you for who you are— and who you're becoming. That kind of external support and validation can make this journey exponentially more rewarding because you get to share it.

Believe it or not, though, not everyone will support you in rewriting your story:

- Some people may feel threatened.

- Some people may have liked you just fine the way you were and not appreciate the fact that you're changing.

- Some people may have benefited from your disempowerment (e.g., taking advantage of you at work or at home) and resent the fact that you're finding your voice and stepping into your strength.

- Some people may have been comfortable with the status quo and not want to rock the boat.

- Some people may have grown accustomed to the "dance" of your relationship or interactions, and when you change your "steps," they're forced to change theirs—or risk getting their toes stepped on!

- Some people might try to lure you back into your old story—through pressure, guilt, anger, shame, derision, or by making fun of you.

So, how do you deal with non-supportive people?

First of all, keep in mind that the changes in your story probably aren't that big a deal to most other people. If you're worried about what others will think (specific people or just the general, vague, and sometimes ominous "They"), let me reassure you: they're probably not thinking about it at all!

This isn't to say you're not important to other people; it's just that they have their own lives, and you're probably not the center of them. This isn't a bad thing, though; in fact, it's incredibly freeing. It means you can just go ahead with your life, your story, and your changes, knowing that the world will keep on turning just as it always has, and "They" will be just fine.

If, however, you encounter people who are truly unsupportive—discouraging, critical, or even nasty—I would recommend that you minimize contact with them. If you can't eliminate them from your life altogether, the less interaction, the better. You've likely have heard that your level of success is the average of the five people you spend the most time with. Well, this includes your success at living your best story. So choose your company wisely and consciously. Make your inner circle a supportive one.

Also, remember that people who try to drag you down—including pressuring you or luring you back into old-story habits—are not true friends. They're like people who offer beer to a recovering alcoholic. They're not keeping your best interests in mind. Fortunately, however, they can't force you back into old habits. But they *can* reinforce your resolve and strengthen your new story and character.

It's natural to want external validation—to be liked, loved, encouraged, and supported for who you are. And it's natural to feel the urge to accommodate, even if that means compromising your values, dimming your light, or playing a role that doesn't reflect your highest self. Yes, some people may think poorly of your new self—thinking things such as, "Who does he think he is?" or "She's getting too big for her britches!" or "That's not the person I used to know" (and mean this in a negative sense). But are you really going to let these unsupportive people dictate the course of your life? Are you going to let the *possibility* that someone might feel threatened by your success keep you from succeeding on *your* terms? Are you going to let the possibility of an occasional negative thought or comment—even from a stranger—keep you from shining?

Remember, what matters isn't what other people think of you but what you think of yourself. (As the saying goes, "What you think of me is none of my business!") They can think what they want—*you're* the one holding the pen, and *you're* the one writing your own story.

Dealing with Difficult People

Have you encountered any resistance to your new character/story? If so, how have you handled these people/situations? What strategies could you use in the future if you encounter unsupportive people?

Surrounding Yourself with Support

How can you surround yourself with supportive people and maximize the percentage of your time you spend with them?

Testing Your Story

Whether it's in the form of temptations (such as beer offered to a recovering alcoholic), criticism from unsupportive so-called friends (or *actual* friends with good intentions but misguided methods), or a nagging internal voice (possibly the lingering words of an old habit dying hard), one thing is certain: *life will test you.*

One person who knows about life's tests firsthand is Barbara, an author in my writing program who has shared her story's ups and downs with me.

Barbara defined herself based on her intelligence. As a teacher, an author, a public speaker, and a therapist, she relied on her mind, and it never seemed to let her down. But that all started to change in 2010 when she was diagnosed with Parkinson's disease.

Suddenly, she experienced bouts of brain fog where she couldn't perform basic mental tasks or remember things she'd known for years. She was frustrated, angry, and afraid—afraid that she was losing her identity and possibly her career. She felt that if people knew about her cognitive impairment, they wouldn't respect her and they certainly wouldn't trust her to be their therapist. So she told almost no one about her condition. Parkinson's became her deep, dark secret—a hidden source of shame.

By the time we met, she'd been telling herself the same story for years: "If people know I have Parkinson's, they won't trust me and they won't want to work with me." But this story wasn't serving her—in fact, it was making her miserable and adding to her already significant struggles. Fortunately, she was open to considering a new story, so we considered alternatives:

What if people respect me even more when they find out I have Parkinson's? What if they admire my persistence in the face of this condition? What if the disease makes me more relatable to others with Parkinson's or to anyone facing significant challenges? Perhaps when they know that, like them, my life hasn't all been smooth sailing, they'll know that I can understand what it's like to struggle. They'll see that health challenges (or other difficult situations) don't necessarily entail the end of your career, your self-esteem, or your life. And maybe they'll actually be more inclined to hire me as their therapist, knowing that I can empathize with their pain and provide hope of a happy, productive, fulfilling life, no matter what obstacles they may face.

Over time, Barbara began to embrace this new perspective. And as she did, she found that it became her reality. She began to speak openly about having Parkinson's. She shared her truth with friends, colleagues, and clients. And now she's even writing a book about her experiences, which she expects will offer insight, understanding, compassion, and hope to those with Parkinson's and their loved ones. Above all, she's released the shame she once felt about this disease, and she feels lighter and freer than she's felt in years.

No, the Parkinson's didn't change, but her story about it did. And that has made all the difference.

Of course, your tests may be very different from Barbara's. Instead of Parkinson's or other health issues, you may face emotional challenges. Or perhaps your boss will ask you to do something that conflicts with your values. Or maybe your new story/self will cause friction in your relationships. But, regardless of your specific situation, one way or another you'll be faced with a choice: move forward with your new-and-improved story or revert to old, unhealthy habits.

The Test Scene

Whether it's in a book, movie, or real life, any story worth its salt contains at least one significant test. For instance, most movies include a "test scene" near the end. This shows that if a character has really changed, they can be put to the test and behave differently than they did (or would have) at the beginning of the film.

For instance, if a character's old pattern was to overeat during times of stress, they may have gorged themselves early in the film. But let's say that they consciously decided to release this pattern and rewrite a new story surrounding food. They go on a diet, lose twenty pounds, and feel great about themselves. They vow that their days of overeating—for comfort during stress or under any other circumstances—are a thing of the past. They've changed their story.

Or so they say…but then comes the test scene. Something very stressful happens in their lives: They're evicted from their apartment. Or their partner breaks up with them. Or they're fired from their job. And then they're left alone with a chocolate cake.

We know that earlier in the film, the cake wouldn't stand a chance—it would be gone within an hour! But if the character has really changed, this time around they won't eat the cake. Sure, they may be tempted. They might even take a bite or two (just enough to make the audience sweat: "Oh no! Are they reverting to their old ways?"). But they won't keep eating. They won't go back to their old story. They'll show that they actually have changed—not just in word but in deed. They're a new character, living a new story.

Test scenes can also show up in your life, and if you're committed to rewriting your story—and actually living it—they almost certainly will. This doesn't mean you're on the wrong path or that you should turn back. It's just a measuring stick of your progress. If you don't initially pass the test, at least it provides feedback about what you'd like to work on. And when you do pass the test, it gives you a chance to congratulate yourself for a true transformation.

Passing the Test

What tests have you faced during this journey of writing, rewriting, and living your story? How did you do? Did it highlight any areas that could still use some work? Or did it show that you've made significant progress?

Case of the Ex

A common test in romantic stories is having the "ex" show up. Even if a protagonist has moved on, an alluring ex can pose a temptation—especially if they try to reignite the old relationship. It's one thing for the protagonist to say, "I've moved on," but quite another to resist a seductive ex. Now *that* is the real test of change.

Even if your story has nothing to do with romantic relationships, you still might be faced with the test of an "ex"—except in your case, it might be an ex-*story!*

Remember in Part II when you wrote a "Dear John" letter to your old story (shortly before you burned it, buried it, or conducted some similar last rites)? Hopefully, this went very smoothly. You were able to express your thoughts and emotions, your displeasure with your soon-to-be-ex-story, and your reasons for breaking up. And then you lit the fire (or flushed the toilet or took out the recycling bin), and that was the end of that.

Forever.

Well, if this had been a real break-up letter to an actual boyfriend or girlfriend, it might not have been so easy—because you would have had another person to contend with. And they might not have left without a fight. Or they might have taken it surprisingly well—perhaps *suspiciously* well—only to show up two weeks later, crying at your doorstep in the middle of the night, begging for you to take them back.

And there's your test scene.

Sometimes tests are easy to pass. For instance, it's not hard to stay broken up with an ex who was disrespectful, manipulative, or just plain bad news—and added nothing positive to your life. But what if they also supported you financially, provided the comfort of the known, or offered other benefits (such as the one that rhymes with "ex")? Or what if there was nothing wrong with them at all; maybe they were good but not good *enough*—not The One?

(In romantic movies, by the way, there's a term for this type: "The Bellamy," named after Ralph Bellamy, who often played dependable but boring characters—guys who didn't necessarily have terrible traits but couldn't hold a candle to his romantic rivals, such as Cary Grant, and failed to ignite the sparks with his love interest. In short, the embodiment of *settling*—a nice-enough guy who might make a good buddy but is hardly Mr. Dream-Come-True.)

Tests can be tricky. (That's why they're called "tests" and not "free passes"!) And any interesting story will make sure that the test scene presents a true challenge—not just an easy, obvious choice. So, although I wish you smooth sailing as you transition into living your new story, I realize that you're likely to face some interesting challenges of your own.

Ideally, once you say goodbye to your old story, that's it...forever! There's also a chance, however, that you may be confronted with a test scene. It may be a full-blown, in-your-face, crying-on-the-doorstep type of moment. (The ex-overeater left alone with the chocolate cake. The recovering alcoholic left alone with a case of vintage wine.) Or it might be something subtler. (The couch-potato-turned-jogger faced with a week of rain. The former procrastinator faced with a deadline.)

Whatever form the test takes, at some point, you'll most likely face this choice: keep living your new story or revert to your old one. Or, to put it in relationship terms: Stay faithful to the new partner or go back to the ex.

What'cha Gonna Do?

In 2000, R&B singer Mýa recorded a song called, "Case of the Ex (What'cha Gonna Do)" in which her partner's ex-girlfriend calls him late at night and invites him over. The singer confronts her partner about the situation, asking, "What'cha gonna do when she wants you back?" (The song also includes the unforgettable closing lyrics: "Yo, playboy right now, uh / Uh, Mýa, think girl, think girl / What what what what uh / Red zone.")

Let's rephrase Mýa's question for our RYS process: "What'cha gonna do when your old story wants you back?" In other words, what if the Part II breakup and funeral don't end up being as final as you'd hoped? What if you find out that your old habits die hard? What if you feel the subtle tug of a "vestigial story," aching like a phantom limb? What if you're tempted to regress? *What'cha gonna do?*

It might seem like there are only two options: You can either stay faithful to the new story, or you can go back to the old one. But there are healthier alternatives. Let's explore a few of them right now.

Notice the Tic Temptation

Since a big goal of this book is to help you live more consciously, one of the most important things you can do is to simply notice when you feel the old story's pull. You might be so accustomed to acting (or reacting) a certain way that your habitual reactions are like reflexive tics. You might see a piece of cake and start eating it before you even realize what you're doing—but that doesn't mean you have to *finish* it! You might see your ex and start flirting (literally or figuratively)—but that doesn't mean you have to move back in together.

Whether or not you act on old-story temptations, just becoming aware of your "tics" or inclinations can help you live more consciously—and steer you in a positive direction.

Feeling Tempted?
Since you've started living your new story, have you felt any old-story temptations? If so, how have they manifested? What did they feel like? Did you find yourself reverting to old habits or reflexive "tics"—or did you simply notice the urge and continue on your new path?

Congratulate Yourself!

If you do feel old temptations, tics, or tendencies starting to resurface—even if you fall off the wagon (that is, temporarily slip back into an old-story habit)—one thing you definitely should *not* do is beat yourself up about it. In fact, I suggest that you do just the opposite: *congratulate yourself!*

Yes, you read that correctly. I think you should congratulate yourself for being aware of how you're feeling or acting. Change starts with awareness, so just by noticing, you've taken the all-important first step. Pat yourself on the back for your awareness, but don't stop there.

Trigger Detection and Redirection

Remember that one of the most habit-forming (and habit-*changing*) tools at your disposal is the trigger—using something as a reminder to launch into a new action. Well, you can use your old-story tics and temptations as triggers, reminding you to take a new-story action. With this approach, those old-story habits don't have to weaken your new story; in fact, they can actually strengthen it.

Once you've become aware of an old-story tic or temptation and decided to use that as your trigger, you have to decide what it's going to trigger. In other words, know how you're going to redirect your attention and your actions. Rather than dwelling on the trigger itself, quickly switch your focus to the new story and take the action you've decided upon in advance.

For instance, if your old habit was to procrastinate by watching TV, you could use the remote control as your trigger. So if you find yourself holding the remote, use that as a reminder to go write (or paint or work out or meditate or whatever your new-story habit is). Or just get up and walk around the house for a few minutes. (Physical movement is one of the best ways to interrupt old-story tics and other patterns—even mental patterns. If you find yourself falling into a disempowering mental loop—such as berating yourself—you can frequently interrupt it simply by physically moving.)

After a few laps up and down the hallway, you might decide that it's okay—you're using TV in a healthy way, such as watching your favorite show as a reward after finishing a big project. (This might be true, but be honest about whose voice you're hearing: Is this your old-story narrator talking? Wait five minutes and ask yourself again.)

So, since you're the "director"—and "redirector"—of your life-movie, how will you redirect yourself if a trigger appears?

Trigger What?

When a piece of your old story pops up, what action will you take? (The action could be an element of your new story, or something as simple as walking into a different room in order to shift your energy/focus. Whatever you do, decide in advance—before you feel old temptations—rather than trying to think clearly while you're in the throes of an old-story tic attack.)

Your New Relationship

Remember, though: redirecting isn't about resisting temptation, fighting your tics and urges, strengthening your resolve, or exercising superhuman willpower (more on that later). It's not about resisting your ex; it's about enjoying your new relationship!

Think of the best beginning of a relationship you've ever experienced: a time when you were head over heels in love, when you got tingly just thinking about the other person, and whenever you were apart all you wanted was to see them again.

When you're in the throes of a full-blown crush like that, you don't have to force yourself to call that person or go see them. In fact, it would probably take more willpower to *stop* yourself from calling or visiting them. They're like a magnet for you. Being together is an absolute joy.

That's what I want your new story to feel like: You *love* it! You can't wait to do your new-story activities, think your new-story thoughts, be your new-story character, and live your new-story life!

So, make your new story as appealing as possible. (And if it's not all that appealing, remember that you can always edit and rewrite it—after all, that's the whole point of this book!) When your new story is a source of immense pleasure for you—when you've got a full-blown crush on this story/character/life—your ex-story won't be able to tempt you away, no matter how hard it tries.

Your New-Story Relationship
The best way to close the door to getting back together with an old, unhealthy ex-story is to form a healthy, fully committed relationship with a consciously created new story. So, what are the most appealing, pleasurable, crush-inducing, commitment-worthy aspects of your new story? How can you focus even more on this new "special someone" in your life? Or, if it's a struggle to focus on your new story, how can you edit the story to make it irresistibly appealing?

The Pleasure Principle, the Myth of Willpower, and the Power of Frames

As I've said, living your new story is not about exercising superhuman willpower to resist your old story. Willpower can only get you so far. You can only force yourself to do something unpleasant for so long until you give it up and go back to your old ways—often with a vengeance. And even if you *could* force yourself to do something unpleasant for the rest of your life, why would you *want* to? Why would you consciously create an unpleasant life?

Either way you look at it, relying on willpower is a losing proposition. On the other hand, when you gain pleasure from doing what serves your highest story/self, it's win-win. The key is to make sure you gain pleasure from living your new story, which you can do in three ways:

- Write a pleasurable story.
- Edit your story to add pleasurable elements (and remove/revise anything unpleasant).
- Reframe it.

Remember our old double-edged friend/foe, reframing? Well, here's where it can really be your friend.

For instance, you might not think that it's pleasurable to pay a bill, but isn't it pleasurable to take another step toward being debt free? I might not find pleasure in exercising, but I sure think it's nice to get healthier. The new painter might not enjoy sitting in traffic, but if she's on her way to buy some canvases, then it's just another part of her very pleasurable story. (Maybe she can use the downtime while stuck in traffic to think of what she wants to paint—or just take a few minutes to relax and enjoy being on her own, sing along with the radio, or simply let her excitement/anticipation build as she slowly makes her way toward the art store.)

Reframing is not lying, and it's not trying to trick yourself into liking something you find thoroughly repulsive. It's about shining a light of truth on why you actually do love and desire something.

I recommend using all three approaches mentioned above: Write a story that's as pleasurable as possible (one that exerts a crush-like magnetic pull on you), keep adding even more pleasurable elements (pile on the appeal and make it a super-sexy story), and then frame it in the most attractive (and truthful) light.

Keep Coming Back to Your Why

Finally, remember your motivation—why you're doing what you're doing: why it's so important, why it will be so pleasant to keep living this story, and why it would be unpleasant (or downright painful) to revert to your old story. Don't be afraid to consider your "away-from" motivations (which can be extremely powerful) but never lose sight of your incredibly positive ultimate goal—and why it will be so great to arrive at your happy ending.

What's Your Why?

What personal motivation is strong enough to keep you coming back to your new story—again and again and again—even in the face of tics, temptations, or old habits? What are your "away-from" motivations (i.e., things you want to avoid by trading in your old life-story for a new one)? And what are your "toward" motivations (i.e., the positive possibilities and experiences that pull you closer to your new story)? Remember why you're doing this—why you were inspired to rewrite your story in the first place, why it's so important to continue the process, and why it's so important to not only write but actually live your new story.

Part IV Summary

The first three parts walked you through the process of identifying your old story, releasing the parts of it you no longer want, and then writing and editing a new story that reflects your highest vision for yourself and your life. Part IV is where this vision comes to life—where you take your story beyond the page and incorporate it into your daily life.

The main elements in this process are:

- *Adaptation* – As you move your story from the page into your real life, you can draw from screenwriting principles, such as cinematography (thinking of how your story might look), showing (rather than just telling), and having a proactive protagonist (namely, taking responsibility for your own life-story rather than waiting for an external *deus ex machina* to save the day).

- *Live Your Story* – Living your story on a day-to-day basis means more than doing something once or twice—it means forming an ongoing habit. To help you ingrain a habit, use a process of clarity, motivation, action, and repetition—and then use "habit helpers" (such as SMART goals, triggers, and accountability partners) to reinforce your new habit/story/life.

- *Life Edits* – Just like you'd edit a written story, you can edit parts of your life, making sure that your words, actions, character, and story are all aligned with your highest values and desires. Edit out anything that tears you down (such as self-deprecating words) and replace it with elements that build you up (such as positive affirmations).

- *Affirmations* – Reinforce your new life-story with affirmations. This can include positive statements about your goal, bridge affirmations (to move you toward that goal), affirmative questions (starting with "What if" or any question with a positive presupposition), and evidence of your success and ability (including positively reframed stories from your past).

- *Reality Check* – As life gives you feedback—from others or from your own inner reactions—take into account the parts that resonate and use those to help you edit, rewrite, and live an even more empowering story.

- *The Company You Keep* – Do everything possible to surround yourself with people who support you, encourage you, and celebrate your new story and your highest self.
- *The Test Scene* – If you feel tempted to slip back into old-story habits, don't worry. Use that awareness to trigger new-story action—and strengthen your "relationship" with your sexy new story.
- *Keep Coming Back to Your Why* – Remember all your personal reasons for rewriting your story, including "toward" motivations (e.g., how you want to feel and what you want to accomplish/experience) and "away-from" motivations (i.e., what you *don't* want in your life).

Looking Forward

In the conclusion, we'll reflect on your RYS journey, consider the big-picture Why of this book/process, and reinforce your commitment to continuing to write and live your ever-evolving masterpiece.

Your Ever-Evolving Masterpiece

[for him]:
Every man is the author of his own life.
The book you are writing is not yet finished.
— Paul Auster

[for her]:
But her story isn't finished,
and for once she's picked up a pen.
— Kelsey Sutton

THROUGHOUT THE *REWRITE YOUR STORY* PROCESS, you've identified, written, explored, released, edited, rewritten, adapted, and lived many stories:

- You identified your old stories and the ones you were still telling yourself when you began reading this book—a process that involved tremendous self-awareness, self-reflection, and a willingness to make the unconscious conscious.

- You explored aspects of your stories that you wanted to keep as is, aspects that you wanted to change, and aspects that you wanted to get rid of altogether—and then you did exactly that!

- You wrote a new story that reflected the best of all worlds—positive elements from your past and present combined with a creative vision for the future, filled with your deepest hopes and desires.

- And then you "told" your story not only through words on a page or thoughts in your head but through your actions—as you adapted your new story into your daily life.

This has been a fairly exhaustive (and perhaps, at times, *exhausting*) process, covering lots of ground and a wide range of stories. But there's one more story that's worth exploring right now: the story of your own journey throughout this process. Like all great stories, this story combines elements that are unique to you and aspects that have been shared by storytellers and heroes since the dawn of time—because, regardless of your specific stories and experiences, throughout the RYS process you've been on a true hero's journey.

Your Heroic Journey

You may already be familiar with the basic structure of The Hero's Journey (which was famously described in Joseph Campbell's *The Hero with a Thousand Faces*), but perhaps you hadn't thought of how it applies to the journey you've been on throughout the RYS process.

In a nutshell, here's the basic structure: A person in their everyday world is called to an adventure. After initial resistance (or flat-out refusal), they meet a mentor who guides them toward their calling. They travel into unknown territory where they face challenges, undergo transformation, and attain a reward. Finally, they return home (which can be an ordeal in itself), bearing the treasure they acquired during their journey, which transforms their "ordinary" world, their lives, and (usually) the lives of those around them.

This journey may be a literal, physical journey or an inner one. It might relate to acts of death-defying bravery or the quiet navigation of a new relationship. The treasure can be a physical "elixir" or new knowledge, perspective, or power.

Although there are as many differences, details, and variations as there are people and journeys in the world, you will almost certainly recognize some pieces of this underlying structure in many of the stories you read and live. In fact, you've probably already taken numerous heroic journeys in many areas of life, and you've certainly taken one while rewriting your story.

This journey started even before you picked up this book: You were just going about your regular life, but you felt called to make a change. Maybe some big external upheaval (e.g., going through a divorce, losing your job, moving, losing a loved one, or experiencing a health crisis) upset your equilibrium, causing you to reevaluate your life. Or maybe you were fed up because your life *wasn't* changing—and the frustration of being stuck in a rut finally overcame the inertia of staying in it. Your personal "inciting incident" may have been loud and dramatic, or maybe you experienced a subtle inner nudge—the "whispers of your soul" inviting you to follow your higher calling.

If you're like most heroes, you probably didn't jump into action the moment you felt the desire to change (or heard the "call to adventure"). You probably resisted, bargained, and hemmed and hawed before finally embarking on a heroic journey of transformation. Maybe you were dragged kicking and screaming (e.g., given an ultimatum by your boss or partner) or maybe you dove willingly into your new adventure, but you almost certainly had encouragement and assistance—such as from a friend, role model, or mentor…which may have taken the form of this book!

As they say, "When the student is ready, the teacher will appear," and you certainly were ready for the next leg of your journey—one that would pull you out of the comfort zone of your "ordinary world" and into the "special world" of adventure and transformation.

Change isn't always easy, though, and you most likely experienced your share of challenges along this journey. In addition to the discomfort that triggered your desire to change, you may have felt discomfort while identifying and exploring your old story—perhaps seeing parts of yourself and your life in an unflattering light. As a true hero, though, you didn't shy away from these revelations. You carried on, deconstructing your old beliefs and patterns, releasing those that no longer served you, and keeping those that do still serve you. Then you took these valuable pieces and combined them with new tools and assets you've picked during this journey, blending them into an empowering new story.

This story is the treasure—the healing "elixir" that will benefit you and those you touch in the "ordinary world" of your everyday experiences. And even though this part of your journey is drawing to a close, you'll continue to apply what you've learned, you'll continue your personal transformation, and you'll continue to benefit others by living your empowered new story.

Reflections on Your Heroic Journey

How does your personal life-story experience correspond to elements of the Hero's Journey? For instance, can you identify your own personal "call to adventure" (in other words, what made you want to read this book and take this journey)? Have you encountered challenges along the way that forced you to change and grow? What treasure have you brought back from this journey (e.g., increased confidence, deepened self-awareness, or greater inspiration to live your dreams)—and how can you continue to use this treasure to enrich your everyday life? How have you and your life changed as a result of this journey?

The Why of Rewrite Your Story

I've repeatedly encouraged you to keep coming back to your Why—your motivation. So, now that we're approaching the end of this book, it seems only fitting that I should tell you my motivations for writing it.

On a personal level, I was tired of procrastinating my life—putting off my biggest dreams. I wanted to get unstuck and reach my goals, such as writing and publishing this book! I hope that by accomplishing this goal, I've not only modeled the RYS process but also inspired you to apply it to your own life, your own goals, and your own story.

Also, I was awed by the power of applying creative-writing tools to real life. I wanted to share these tools, provide guidance on how to use them effectively, and encourage you to use them not just once (while reading this book) but again and again and again—whenever you want to, for your entire life.

But perhaps above all else, I wrote this book because I wanted to rewrite the story I told in the introduction—the story of the seven-year-old driving the car of your life. This is a terrible story, and I'd seen it told (and lived) again and again, as people (including myself) let their childhood stories dictate their adult lives. Watching these disempowering stories get acted out felt like watching an accident waiting to happen or, more accurately, an accident in progress—which makes sense given that a seven-year-old was driving! In the "lucky" cases, the childhood story wouldn't cause a disaster but would merely get people stuck in a rut, spinning their wheels around and around the same ground for years without making forward progress, but this was hardly a victory! I knew that it didn't have to be this way—that there was a way out of this rut, a way to prevent accidents, and a way to move forward with our lives. And that's the main reason why I wrote this book: to help us all ease the pain and end the frustration caused by these outdated stories—and to reclaim our power as storytellers of our own lives.

Just because a seven-year-old has been driving the car of your life doesn't mean you have to let them continue driving. And just because someone told you a disempowering story when you were seven (or three, thirteen, nineteen, or any other impressionable age) doesn't mean that has to be your story for life. You can reclaim the wheel, reclaim the pen, become the empowered author of your own story, and turn your life into an ever-evolving masterpiece!

Your Ever-Evolving Masterpiece

In the coming days, weeks, months, and years, I hope you'll continue to incorporate the lessons from this book for different parts of your life-story: *Identify*, *Release*, *Rewrite*, and *Live*. In other words, notice aspects of your life that you'd like to change, consciously let go of the disempowering (or simply not-enjoyable or not-you) aspects, write a new story that reflects your new goals and ideals, and then incorporate that new story into your daily life.

And remember that you can always edit, revise, and rewrite your story. Throughout your life, your story will continue to change because *you* will continue to change. But now you're no longer at the mercy of these changes because you have the tools to consciously create the future (and present) you want. I hope you'll continue to use these tools for the good of yourself, others, and the world. And I hope you'll continue to enjoy the glorious experience of being the empowered author of your own life.

About the Author

People think that stories are shaped by people.
In fact, it's the other way around.
— Terry Pratchett

D AN TECK HAS DIVIDED HIS PROFESSIONAL LIFE between personal growth and writing. He's a Certified Life-Optimization Coach, a Certified Law of Attraction Master Practitioner, and a bestselling author. He received a BA in Religious Studies from Vassar College and an MFA in Creative Writing from Mills College and has spent over thirty years studying, practicing, and teaching a wide variety of spiritual paths and personal-growth techniques.

In addition to his own books, he's also the author of the personal-growth blog *Halfway up the Mountain* as well as the co-creator (with his wife, Jodi Chapman) of the bestselling *365 Book Series* and *Soulful Journals Series*, numerous personal-growth ecourses, and the Your Soulful Book writing program. Through his books, courses, and communities, Dan has helped thousands of people rewrite their stories and create their own happy endings (and middles and "right-nows")—and he feels blessed to help you do the same.

If you enjoyed this book, please leave a positive Amazon review, which will help others to rewrite their stories, improve their lives, and spread the love.

Soulful Journals by Jodi Chapman & Dan Teck

Jodi and Dan are updating their *Soulful Journals Series*, which includes the following titles that are already published or that will be published soon:

- *As If – A Manifestation Journal: Visualize Your Ideal Life & Make Your Dreams Come True*

- *Bring Your Dreams to Life: Discover Your Soul's Purpose & Turn Your Visions into Reality*

- *The Gratitude Journal: Prompts & Activities to Get the Grateful Feelings Flowing…in Just Minutes a Day!*

- *Journaling Within: Soulful Writing Prompts to Help You Discover Your True Self*

- *Journaling Within for Teens: Soulful Questions to Help You Get to Know Yourself*

- *The Joy Journal: Soulful Prompts & Activities to Help You Bring More Happiness into Your Life*

- *Self-Care from the Inside Out: Helpful Ways to Give Yourself the Love You Deserve*

- *Transitions: Soulful Prompts to Guide You Through Life's Changes*

For additional information and updates, and to pick up your free *The Joy of Joy* meditation + activity book, please visit: www.soulfuljournals.com.

Tomorrow, in a very real sense, your life—the life you author from scratch—
begins.... Build yourself a great story.
— Jeff Bezos

Made in the USA
Monee, IL
15 October 2022